THE GOLDEN STATE KILLER

PETE DOVE

The End To Decades of Terror?

They were some of the coldest, most savage crimes in the entire history of the United States; murder, rape, assault and burglary. Victims were tracked and stalked; the violations committed against them vicious and merciless. Men, women, children; none were safe from his deadly attacks.

But the Golden State Killer, as he came to be known, had another wicked, callous side. Not only would he destroy his victims' lives, but he would then taunt them, make them relive what they had been through with phone calls that would impart even more terror.

We do not know the motivation of the man who carried out these crimes, and perhaps never will. Sexual gratification? But that does not take account of the murders, often of male partners. This was a killer who did not particularly seek out single women, at least, not later in his campaign. Power? Maybe, perhaps there was a perverse thrill to be had in demonstrating total control over his helpless victims. Mental illness? It is hard to imagine a person carrying out the terrible actions of the Golden State Killer being of sound mind. But insanity is not absolute. It exists on a wide spectrum and the overwhelming majority of sufferers, in whatever form they experience mental illness, manage their condition. And a person who is completely insane does not stop; he has no control over their wickedness. But the Golden State Killer did stop; he did plan his crimes with attention to detail, he did change the location of his attacks through the time of his spree. Perhaps he is a man of pure evil. Such people do exist, and sometimes opportunity arises for them to carry out their warped desires, to perpetrate the malevolence within.

For many years it seemed as though we would never know. But now a man has been arrested and charged with the crimes committed many years ago. He is yet to face trial, and he is (at the time of writing) yet to enter a plea. We must, in the interests of justice and a fair trial, assume that Joseph James DeAngelo is innocent until proven otherwise, or until he admits his guilt. Imagine carrying the weight of such accusations as are made against this person if they are innocent.

Defence Counsel believes it will be several months, perhaps even years, before the case can come before a court, such is the weight of evidence to be examined, questioned and ratified. Let us hope that this does not become a case tried by media, or expediated for political benefit. The victims – many alive, many dead – of the killer need to know the truth and be confident with it. That takes time, fairness and an open mind.

The Background

Jane Carson was an early victim of the Golden State Killer, although, in those days he was referred to as the East Side Rapist (even, sometimes, the Original Night Stalker). As yet, killings were not on his agenda. Jane lived in Citrus Heights, close to Sacramento. It was the first home she had ever owned. The neighborhood was quiet and friendly. Jane was thirty when the assault took place. She had a small, blond three-year-old son, and was married to a military officer. Her own career was taking off, and she was studying for a nursing degree. Early in the morning, she would become his fifth victim. It was 6.30 in the morning of October 5th, 1976, and Jane heard the garage door close, telling her that her husband had left for work. Within minutes, she heard footsteps. On this occasion the attacker carried a butcher knife. Her son was snuggled next to Jane, and the killer tied both of them up, blind folding them and stuffing rags into their mouth.

'It's hard to describe, especially with your three-year-old lying next to you. It's hard to describe the fear,' explained the woman, years later.

He untied Jane's ankles, and she knew what was going to happen. She went to touch her son, to reassure him, but he was gone. Jane was consumed by fear, for her son, for herself.

The rapist went into the kitchen, rattling pots and pans, working through her fridge. Throughout the ordeal, he would return to the bedroom threatening to kill Jane should she make a sound. In fact, she believed he was there for two hours before he left quietly, having put back Jane's son beside her. It was a unique way of operating. Usually, rapists would enter through an unlocked door or window, carry out their assault and leave quickly, sometimes taking cash or jewelry. Sometimes, this man would go quiet, and his victims would think he had left. They would move, but he would still be there, threatening once more.

Over forty years after the event, Jane is still affected. Now she wants answers to questions, such as how long her attacker had stalked her, how he entered the home. Perhaps, if DeAngelo is the killer, she may find out these answers in the coming months.

Jane's evidence, and that of other victims, began to help police develop a picture of the perpetrator. They were looking for a man between 5' 8" and 5' 10" tall, weighing around one hundred and sixty-five pounds. He was athletically built; his age estimated as being between eighteen and thirty.

Victims reported another particularly interesting physical attribute of their attacker. They described a man with an especially small penis. Could that have been a factor in his need to spread a blanket of terror? Was it a way of the killer countering something that caused him deep personal anxiety?

Another peculiarity about this particular predator was the speed with which he struck in those first years. At times, crimes would be taking place weekly. Carol Daly is a retired police officer, who worked on some of the early assaults and followed the cases closely. She tells of another aspect to his modus operandi, something that became clearer to police the longer his crimes spree continued. It helped them to build up a picture of the man they were seeking.

'He always stole something,' said Daly, 'there were driver's licences, there were photos there was money, there was jewellery.'

He would also take credit cards, or other items from his victims' wedding. He had a fondness for personal items, such as photos and objects bearing the name of those he attacked. Although he wore gloves, he did leave clues behind. He liked to make himself at home and would often eat or drink his victim's food and drink. On one occasion police found a Pepsi can left outside.

It also seems as though this was a rapist with an ego. A report in a Sacramento newspaper states that he never attacks a woman when a man is present. And from then on, in about two out of every three of the assaults he carries out, a man is present.

Carol Daly explains how he operated when a man was present. 'It was very sadistic. The male victims were tied up laying on their stomachs with their hands tied behind their back and their feet tied.' He would often get the man's partner to do the binding, before tying up the subject of his sexual assault. The attacker would go to the kitchen and collect plates and dishes, which he would place on the man's back, telling him that he would hear if the man moved. The woman would then be led to another room, raped and assaulted. The emotional pain of hearing a loved one being attacked while you can do nothing is hard to imagine. And, he was quite prepared to enter homes where there were children, who too would hear what was going on, but could do nothing about it. Such trauma lasts forever.

In a frighteningly bizarre way, it is possible that the Sacramento news article was interpreted by the attacker as an assault on his own abilities, his own manhood. If this is a man already deeply disturbed, such a report could have led him to vary the targets of his crimes.

In the first year of his crime spree, twenty-two attacks take place. And those are just the ones about which the police know. Carol Daly tells of how the barbarism of some of his assaults would leave victims too ashamed to come forward. Rapes were not just vaginal penetrations but included oral attacks and deviant sexual acts.

Jane Carson said: 'Sacramento was in a state of fear.' Women were locking their windows, double checking that their doors were secure. Police advised getting to know neighbour's habits, so that anything unusual could be reported as soon as it was spotted. Gun sales went up, and an unexpected consequence was that burglary rates in Sacramento plummeted. Robbers knew the risk of getting shot made it not worthwhile to break into somebody's home. Public meetings were held to calm and advise the community. Women were told that if they were attacked, they had to injure their attacker sufficiently badly to incapacitate him. Vigilante rule was close to hitting the streets of the usually calm Californian city.

At one meeting, a frightening and bizarre series of consequences was set in motion. A man stood up to say that he could not believe that the attacker could get away with his crimes when there was more than one person in the house. The rapist could be dealt with by the man. It seems as though the killer must have been present, and just as with the newspaper report that he saw as a challenge, so he saw the man's comments as an insult to his manhood. A few months later, the man who had spoken out and his wife became one of the Golden State Killer's victims. The attack on them was one of the most vindictive of the campaign.

And it also suggested that the perpetrator was there, among that community, hiding in plain sight. The particular area of Sacramento on which he preyed was a middle-class suburb, and his comfort in those areas suggests that he, too, was from a middle-class upbringing, or lived among such people at that time. He knew how to dress, what car to drive, how to carry himself so that he did not bring any attention upon himself.

His Victims

DeAngelo was living in the neighbourhood where many of his alleged crimes took place when he was arrested towards the back end of April 2018. Citrus Heights is a pleasant, middle class part of California. But in the late 1970s and 1980s is was a community living in fear. Linda O Dell was yet another victim of the killer. She was raped at knife point, while her husband was tied up and unable to help. Just twenty-two at the time, Linda felt ashamed about the attack. This was the 1980s and understanding of the trauma felt by victims was not well developed. She tells of there being little empathy from police, and little support for her after the attack.

Her sister had to move in with her because she was terrified of being alone, when her husband went to work. The rapist had demanded her wedding and engagement rings, in between drinking beer from her kitchen. He had threatened to cut off her fingers if she could not remove them. The emotional scars she bore would not readily heal.

But later Linda joined the Me Too movement, a support group for victims. It empowered her and has helped her move forwards in her life. 'I felt judged,' she recalls. 'I didn't feel like a victim back ten. I didn't want people to know it about me.'

In 1977, Margaret Wadlow was living in the pleasant Sacramento suburbs. She was just thirteen, and both fascinated and frightened by the growing number of attacks taking place nearby. However, her mother, who was then 55, tried to be reassuring. Up to that point, there had been no killings, and the rapes tended to be carried out on young women. 'You're too young and I'm too old,' Margaret recalls her mother telling her. Unfortunately, on this occasion, mother's judgement was wrong.

One night in November Margaret woke suddenly to see a flashlight in her face. In her mid-sleep stupor, she initially thought it was a neighbour playing a practical joke, but that feeling rapidly passed and she knew that he East Area Rapist, as he was still known at that time, was the man whispering angrily and standing before her.

Despite her young years, Margaret suspected that it was the fear he instilled in his victims that gave the rapist most pleasure. She was determined to deny him that. When he asked her whether she wanted him to kill her, and her mother, she replied 'I don't car.' As when he had attacked homes with men sleeping next to their wives, he tied up her mother and placed plates and dishes on her back, so he would hear if she moved. He then raped the young girl.

The attack was quickly over, but as was his wont the attacker stayed in the house for more than an hour. When he finally left, Margaret recalls her mother shouting for help, waiting for neighbours to hear.

Ironically, a couple of years later, the mother and daughter moved to Orange County, California. That would soon become one of the locations for his next series of attacks. For Margaret, holding on to her experiences has been her therapy. She has never spoken to a professional about her trauma and should DeAngelo prove to be the culprit, it will move her life onto another phase. Hopefully one that is better still. However, her refusal to admit her fear to her rapist has been a source of comfort to her.

'I always felt that I triumphed. I felt like I controlled what happened as much as I could,' she says of the dreadful night. 'I had influence over that night. I felt like I was the victor, and I have always gone with that.'

While he had not killed any victims, as far as police knew at that time, up to the point of the attack on Margaret, this was something soon to change. Up to the murders of Katie and Brian Maggiore in Rancho Cordova during the night of February 2nd 1978, the attacker had satisfied himself with instilling fear and horror through rape and sexual assault.

Prior to his first murders police believe that the East Area Rapist was responsible for thirty rapes, and one attempted sexual assault. Six had been in Rancho Cordova, nine in Carmichael. The same number had been committed in Sacramento itself, and Citrus Heights had seen three attacks, and there had been one in Stockton and two in Orangevale. But later that figure increased. At the time of writing, and police are aware that the publicity at the moment might draw other victims out from under the cloak of fear and shame, the East Area Rapist has been linked to fifty rapes between 1976 and 1986, plus they have found DNA evidence linking him to the deaths of ten victims, with another three likely to have been murdered by him. And he was targeting areas further north. Now Modestor, Davis, Concord and San Jose were subjected to his reign of terror. As were Goleta, Ventura, Walnut Creek, San Ramon and Danville.

But that night in February, close to the Rancho Cordova Home of Brian and Katie Maggiore, his crimes escalated to a new level. Initially, the murder of the couple was not associated with the other crimes police had linked together. The couple were walking their dog, when they were confronted by an armed man. They ran, and Brian was chased into a neighbour's backyard, where he was shot in the chest. Katie almost made it home, she was killed by the gate to her house.

There was no rape, no sexual assault, and of course there had been no killings, despite the many threats to the contrary. Perhaps he had been disturbed undertaking the intelligence observations he must have carried out before committing his crimes. Perhaps he planned to attack in the open air, and it simply went wrong. Whatever, it would be his penultimate crime in the southern part of Sacramento county. He committed another rape, this time in on a young, fifteen-year-old babysitter in April. Then he moved north.

Nobody is sure of the reason for this. But perhaps he felt that the police were closing in. Witness statements had enabled the authorities to put together a composite picture of the Maggiores' killer. Perhaps that illustration was accurate, a good likeness that could see him recognised.

On moving north, his MO seemed to change. No longer did he base his crimes in a relatively narrow band of the state. Now he switched between Modesto and Davis, and committed five attacks, at least, in a two-month period in the summer of 1978. Next, his choice of location changed once more, with another seven attacks, maybe more if further victims come forward, in the Contra Costa County region over the next nine months. In an attack on July 5th 1979, a vital clue emerged.

The East Side Rapist had broken into a house in Danville, but the husband was a light sleeper, and woke as the serial killer was putting on his ski mask. He was able to confront the rapist who panicked, and fled the scene, but his face had been seen, albeit briefly. For the calculating criminal, the risk of returning to that area was now too great, and he chose yet another area to terrorise.

Mistakes were creeping into his acts. Perhaps he was becoming over confident, or his luck was just running out. Many criminal psychologists believe that a high percentage of serial attackers have within them a wish to stop their reign of terror, but their compulsion is too strong. These rapists and killers subconsciously realise that the only way they can stop is to be caught, and therefore they take increasingly dangerous risks. We do not know that caused the East Side Rapist to morph into a killer, but in October 1979, one of his attacks went very wrong.

The victims were Mary Brown and her partner John Davis. The attack followed the usual pattern, during the attacker's periodic ransacking runs through the house, Mary Brown escaped, hopping to the front door and screaming for help. She was caught and dragged back into the house. Meanwhile, Davis escaped the other way, into the backyard. The rapist turned his attentions back to the man, and Brown escaped once more, this time running into a neighbour who had been awoken by her screams. The attacker panicked and fled the scene on a bicycle.

For John Davis and Mary Brown their ordeal was over, the physical part at least, but the rapist apparently realised that he needed to do something more to stop his attacks from going wrong again. He had already killed once, at least, and decided that murder would provide the answer to his problems.

At the end of December 1979 Robert Offerman and Debra Alexandria would become his next murder victims. They lived just a couple of blocks away from his failed attack on Mary Brown and John Davis. Evidence suggests that Robert managed to free himself from his bonds and attack the rapist. He was shot to death, and Debra was executed straight after. The shots were heard, but so close to New Year celebrations, neighbours thought the bangs were firecrackers let off a night too early.

A couple of months later Lyman and Charlene Smith were killed. The method employed this time was different, the couple being bludgeoned to death with a log from a fireplace. Charlene had been raped. In August 1980, Keith and Patrice Harrington were killed in the same way as the Smiths. Once more, the woman had also been raped. Six months passed before the next murder. It seems as though the killer had by now settled upon his new M.O., dispatching his victims by hitting them with a blunt instrument. Another attack saw Manuela Witthuhn raped. Her husband was away at the time of the assault, something that must haunt him for the remainder of his days.

Debbi Domingo is another victim whose life has been indelible marked by the Golden State Killer. She was fifteen when a row with her mother led her to storm out of the house in a teenage rage. She stayed with friends for two weeks before a call brought her home. There she found police tape sealing the house, and inside were the bodies of her mother, thirty-five-year-old Cheri, and her boyfriend Gregory Sanchez, who was just twenty-seven. Their murders were so savage that police initially could not identify the bodies. Once more, they had been assaulted with a blunt weapon, which was removed from the crime scene, but Gregory Sanchez had also been shot in the face.

The first suspect was Debbi's father, who was thought to have carried out some kind of revenge attack. However, it was soon clear that he was not involved in the murder. The impact on Debbi led her to move to the world of citizen sleuths, members of the public who try to put together the solutions to unsolved crimes. The growth of social media made the task easier, and soon a group were looking into the murder of her mother.

Positive action has been therapeutic for Debbi, and the recent arrest of DeAngelo has helped a little further. The pain will never go away, but closure may be round the corner.

'We just did not give hope. To see that the DNA matches came through,' she said 'and that they have him in custody. That's what we were all praying for.

May 4th 1986 saw his last confirmed victim raped and murdered. Janelle Lisa Cruz was home alone while her family were in Mexico on vacation. She was raped and bludgeoned to death, most probably with a pipe wrench from her washing machine.

Of course, back in the 1970s and 1980s, DNA evidence was still in its infancy. There were two apparently serial criminals operating in the California region. The first, who burgled and raped, was known as the Original Night Stalker, the second, the East End Rapist. But DNA links made in 2001 showed that this was the same person. This made the man California's most 'prolific serial offender.' It was apparent that he was a killer and rapist who operated across more than just the East Side, who did more than just stalk at night, as awful as these crimes might be. A new name was coined for him, coined by a woman who dedicated her life to identifying this killer. We will learn more about her later. This was where the sobriquet Golden State Killer originated.

He may also have been the perpetrator of the 'Vinsalia Ransacker' case, when in 1975 Claude Snelling was murdered and an attempt was made to kidnap his daughter. He may have been responsible for other murders, for other rapes and for other sexual crimes. Burglary, it seems may have brought about his introduction into crime. As yet, facts remain uncertain, the full picture cloudy, but with more than fifty victims, nobody would disagree that this is a man who needs to be brought to justice.

The Investigation

Paul Holes is a cold case investigator and has visited every single crime scene associated with the East Area rapist. 'You almost have a personal obligation – you've got to catch this guy now. This is one of the worst serial predators that I'm aware of,' he says.

It appears that the rapist has far better than expected intelligence about many of these locations, even as far as knowing what is going on in the houses of his victims.

The ninth attack, on November 10th 1976, illustrates this point. It is 6.30 in the evening and a teenage girl is left at home. She is due to go out with her boyfriend before her parents are expected back. The girl is dragged outside and tied up. But then the rapist returns to the house, and makes it look like the girl has left naturally. He next takes her two hundred yards away down a nearby canal, where he can have time with her.

When her parents return home, they have no idea that anything is wrong. Paul Holes believes he is a very organized offender, who possibly even took notes about the sites of his crimes, possibly stalking numerous locations at one time.

Then, in 2015, the FBI refueled public interest by offering a $50000 reward for information leading to the capture of the Golden State Killer. The case was back in the public eye, and the net was tightening.

But from the outset, it was not just the police who have shown an interest in this case. Michelle McNamara published a book on the crimes, and we will look in more detail at her findings later. Other 'citizen sleuths' have also been involved.'

Mike Morford is a true crime blogger. Keith Komos is a website developer, but also follows the case. Police find their help often useful. Citizen sleuths often work together, collaborating to maximize their effectiveness.

One occasion a badge was discovered, in 1978 and this was released to the public. It could have been dropped by the East Area Rapist. A seven-point star is emblazoned around the side, and State of California is engraved in the center. It seems to suggest somebody with a career in law enforcement, or something similar. DeAngelo was a policeman for a short time.

Indeed, the idea that the rapist could have been a police officer was a consideration from the very start of the investigation. This person seemed to know everything that was going on. Patrol officers were employed, wearing plain clothes, in the Rancho Cordova area where many of the attacks took place. In that area, there are only four places to cross the river back into the main part of Sacramento, and surveillance cars were situated on these bridges in the hope that, when a call came in, they could catch the perpetrator fleeing the area. These approaches were never successful, which offered a hint at least that the rapist was aware of the police department's actions.

Attacks were carefully planned, and the criminal appeared to have great physical dexterity – sometimes police thought that they spotted him, but he always escaped, leaping fences and racing through people's gardens. Both of these skills could have been learned on professional courses, the sort of tactical training regularly undertaken by police officers.

Another attack was being planned in February 1977. But on this occasion, the rapist ran into a seventeen-year-old cross-country runner called Rodney Miller: Rodney's mother saw a man in her garden, and called Rodney, who went to chase him. Rodney closed him down, but as agile as he might be, Rodney was a good athlete and soon caught him. The attacker fell, and as Rodney was about to apprehend him, he shot the young man in the stomach.

It was clear that the rapist had spent some time in the area, a footprint matching that of the East Side Rapist was discovered, and imprints were discovered in a patch of ivy. To Rodney's mother, it is clear that the attacker was a trained man, because he had skills that most people simply do not possess.

Although DeAngelo had police training, before his arrest police also considered that their subject could have been a military man. Five of the first sixteen assaults took place close to an airbase, across the freeway from

Mather(?) air force base. The attacker was comfortable with firearms, and of course the fifth attack was on the wife of an air force captain. He was frequently reported as wearing military boots.

Keith Komos and Mike Morford continued to investigate a star shaped badge police had discovered near one of the crime scenes. It certainly bore similarities to official hardware issued by the State but did not match exactly with anything. Then an expert on Californian badges got in touch and identified the object immediately. Keith explained that it was neither a valuable, nor especially common badge. 'It was used,' he revealed 'by at best, a security guard. No law enforcement officer would have a badge like this.'

Something DeAngelo's defense attorney will no doubt make great play about when the cases come to trial. But although useful, the finding is not definitive. The badge could be completely unrelated to any attack.

And for Paul Holes, although he suspects the man could have had military training – he could have been of an age where national service was commonplace, and the Vietnam War was at its height, he does not find any overwhelming evidence that the killer was associated with the police force. However, that does not mean that he was not.

The investigation does suggest that the attacker might have planted mis-information that would be easily accessed by police and could lead them away from the truth. For example, he says to some victims 'Don't tell the pigs you saw my van outside.' He knows that they would then report that their attacker drove a van. Perhaps even the badge was planted, bought from a memorabilia store or a garage sale, and deliberately dropped near a scene of a crime to lead police towards the conclusion that their man was a security guard.

Carol Daly, the retired detective, kept the case alive, keeping a detailed file of confidential information. She focused on the early cases, when he was known as the East Area Rapist. She was able to bond to the victims, get them to talk about what had happened to them. But it took to the fourth or fifth victim before it became apparent that there was a pattern.

Carol Daly tells of his method. He would wait at the bottom of the bed, where his victim was sleeping. He would shine a flashlight in their eyes, so when they awoke he would be in shadow, a frightening sight. He carried a gun and wore a ski mask. He enjoyed, it seemed, carrying out his crime. He would move back and forth, entering and leaving the room, tormenting his victim. Then the rape would begin with other sexual assaults taking place. He spoke to his victim through clenched teeth, using a hoarse whisper, telling them not to move, or make a sound. If they did, he would kill them. The fear was absolute.

She also believed that somebody knew about him. The police had a detailed description, they could produce a photo-fit picture, they even knew his shoe size. He stole trinkets from his victim's homes. He mixed easily in the community. A girlfriend, a mother or a colleague surely knew who he was.

The Lucky Break

When the breakthrough finally came, it was from a source nobody could have predicted. A distant relative of DeAngelo had an interest that is shared by millions across the US, and indeed the rest of the world. They were searching for their family ancestry. Companies such as Ancestry.com and 23andMe provide DNA sample kits which can be completed by the person conducting the search to offer a wider base for their search. However, these major firms require a court order to be in place for the authorities to scroll through their massive genetic databases.

But the public ancestry site. GEDmatch works differently. It offers a free service of which t the relative of DeAngelo was taking advantage. This widely used tool allows the public to upload the DNA profiles they have found through the testing kits they got from other suppliers, and so widen their search further. The investigation now reaches a legal point that could well form a key part of the case to come. While the authorities had no court order to scan through the wide database held by GEDmatch, a phishing search in which they hoped to find links to a wide range of current and cold case crimes, the police claim that, because the data is already available to the public, they did not need additional authority to carry out their search.

What the case might do for GEDmatch's public profile is hard to predict. On the old adage that any publicity is good publicity they may find their profile raised, and business flooding towards them. But while most Americans would agree that the perpetrators of crime should be identified and brought to justice, many users are going to have concerns. Firstly, where their DNA offers a close match to samples held by the police in their investigations, they will be subjecting themselves and close family members to potential scrutiny. Some will say they have nothing to hide, and if it helps the interests of justice then such examination sits comfortably with them. Others will be reluctant to think that they are being quietly investigated, and probably do not know about it. A third group might just hold suspicions that they could inadvertently bring down their families if an unsuspected link is found.

For their part, GEDmatch feel that the matter has been taken out of their hands. They issued a statement which said: "It has always been GEDmatch's policy to inform users that the database could be used for other uses, as set forth in the Site Policy. While the database was created for genealogical research, it is important that GEDmatch participants understand the possible uses of their DNA, including identification of relatives that have committed crimes or were victims of crimes. If you are concerned about non-genealogical uses of your DNA, you should not upload your DNA to the database and/or you should remove DNA that has already been uploaded.'

But, as we all know, there is a world of difference between a statement in the lengthy terms and conditions of a service to which we all sign at one time or another, usually without reading (they stretch to thousands of words for a reason!) and seeing the impact of those conditions revealed so publicly.

There will be further concerns about the ways in which the impact of this such high-profile case could lead to future law changes. If the case proves to be successful, and the arrest comes about because of the distant relative's use of a public website, many will suspect pressure could be applied to allow the authorities to use the genetic data held by commercial companies far more widely, and without the necessary court order. That would lead to the kind of random phishing which a lot of people feel becomes an invasion of their civil liberties, a 'big brother' action more normally associated with Soviet era Russia or North Korea than a free, capitalist and liberal state. Even where we currently stand, it is unclear whether GEDmatch was the only database police searched. The Sacramento County District Attorney's office refused to comment of the breadth of their investigations, from which we must draw the conclusions we will. If the DA's office wants the public to believe their police's search was restricted to one site, then that is something they need to confirm. What we do know, however, is that GEDmatch themselves are denying that they gave any permission for the data they held to be investigated. They issued a statement refuting any knowledge of the police department's actions. Other ancestry sites also confirmed that they had not been approached by the authorities.

Equally, DeAngelo is yet to even face trial let alone be convicted. It is hard to see quite how he can have a fair trial when there is such publicity surrounding his position. If it turns out that he has been falsely accused, is innocent of these appalling crimes, the impact on people prepared to use such sites will be severely affected.

Once the police's general search of GEDmatch's database of DNA had thrown up a link with the DNA held in the Golden State Killer case, the next stage was to investigate family members to find out if any matched the age profile and the residential location that could make them strong suspects. It was after this stage that DeAngelo's name began to look promising.

Police next obtained – they are yet to say how – a current DNA sample. When they sent this for testing, the results came back positive. They repeated the process, desperate to make doubly sure that they were not about to commit the unforgiveable act of wrongly accusing a man of these appalling crimes. The second sample came back positive. The police acted quickly, DeAngelo was arrested and the world took notice.

The entire legal position is foggy. 23andMe stated that they resist law enforcement enquiries, feeling that they have a duty to protect customers" privacy. '23andMe has never given customer information to law enforcement officials,' they stated.

Ancestry.com operates a slightly more bespoke policy. While it 'advocates for its members' privacy' it has cooperated with previous police investigations. Most notoriously, it worked alongside police who were attempting to track down a man in Idaho who had raped and killed a woman. The genealogy company publishes an annual report identifying occasions where it had worked with police. That report shows that last year Ancestry.com was approached for help on 34 occasions and agreed on 31 of those. These are, of course, cases where the police enquiries are not backed by a court order.

Some doubts also exist over the efficacy of linking police held DNA records and those collected by the genealogy companies. These records come from collections of saliva, which is very rarely found and collected at crime scenes. It is another point on which the defense may come to rely when the case comes to trial.

As things stand, it looks as though legally the police will be found to be correct in their belief. It appears to be true that the law allows them to use DNA found on public sites as they wish. However, many believe there is a moral question here, with most people who use the sites being completely unaware of the potential impacts of their actions. They neither consider nor know about the risks they may be subjecting family members to by using the sites.

Steve Mercer is the chief attorney in the forensic division of the Maryland Office of the Public Defender and, like many others, he is deeply concerned by the latest developments.

'People who submit DNA for ancestors testing are unwittingly becoming genetic informants on their innocent family, who have fewer privacy protections than convicted offenders whose DNA is contained in regulated databanks.'

The Amateur Investigator

For comedian Patton Oswalt the arrest of Joseph James DeAngelo has been bittersweet. It was his wife who came up with the name the killer and rapist was known by, the Golden State Killer. And it was his wife who dedicated much of her life to investigating, researching and chronicling what happened during that dreadful decade in California.

Michelle McNamara was an investigative journalist, a writer with an interest in true crime, and a natural empathy with many of its victims. Unlike some, she was a generous investigator, happy to share and collaborate with others as she strode towards her ultimate objective. This was not to make a fortune with a best-selling book, but to identify the culprit behind those sordid acts and help the police to bring him to justice.

McNamara was just 46 when she died in her sleep, of unidentified causes, in April 2016. Her constant travel, and the regular stresses of meeting with victims and viewing crime scenes probably played their part in her early death. Certainly, her still devastated husband believes so.

It was an irony that the book she wrote to help identify the killer became the best seller she had not sought. But by then she had passed on, and the book had been finished by her friends and collaborators.

With a degree of churlishness not uncommon of the US Police, the Sacramento County Sherriff, Scott Jones, refused to credit McNamara's work with leading to their solving of the crime. Keen to take his moment in the spotlight, it appeared, he responded to the question over the help the book had provided by saying: 'No. It kept interest in tips coming in. other than that, there was no information extracted from the book that directly led to the apprehension. There will be many who see a direct contradiction in that statement.

One final twist suggests that there might be some kind of almost metaphysical link between the book and the arrest. Just two hours before the news broke that DeAngelo had been arrested, the team behind the book, including Oswalt, were taking place at a promotion to keep the case in the public eye. They were also on the first day of filming a new documentary about the case.

Coincidence? Probably, but a strange one nevertheless.

The Suspect

Judy Gelein was one of Joseph James DeAngelo's alleged victim. She told the East Bay Times that 'he's always been a Bogeyman and today I see the Bogeyman is real.' To many observers, the syllables 'Bogey' could better be replaced with the words 'frail' and 'old', judging by his short appearance in court. Yet still the impact of that criminal on the lives of his victims, their friends and families, cannot be underestimated. If still alive, that man is now elderly – he might or might not be Joseph DeAngelo. Most will believe though, that old age cannot mask the consequences of his past actions.

'Me and my husband slept with our windows open for the first time in 42 years,' said Judy Gelein.

Balding, blotchy and seemingly weak, DeAngelo could hardly speak at his arraignment. He answered his name, his voice barely carrying, it's raspy tone echoing to the terrifying phone calls the rapist made to his victims so many years ago. He answered that he had a lawyer; a public defender, Diane Howard has been assigned to represent the man.

He has yet to enter a plea.

Clearly, many members of the press felt that DeAngelo was overplaying his poor health. Howard was asked repeatedly to confirm that he needed a wheel chair, but at the time of writing she would be drawn on nothing to do with the case.

Nevertheless, the sight of an elderly man – DeAngelo is 72, manacled to a wheel chair does no society good. Mahatma Gandhi said that 'The true measure of any society can be found in how it treats its most vulnerable members.' Without passing judgement on the guilt or otherwise of DeAngelo and the extent to which his alleged crimes make him forfeit the normal rights of humanity, at present he is innocent, and is so until he is found guilty, he is clearly vulnerable and to chain such a person to a chair is, to most right-thinking people, unacceptable.

Since his arrest he has spoken to nobody and accepted no visits. He has been reclusive, and is on suicide watch, such is the concern for his safety.

On the other hand, the wickedness of the crimes he is alleged to have carried out can never be overstated.

DeAngelo spent several years of his early working life as a policeman. He served the town of Exeter, which is to the south of Sacramento, from 1973 to 1976. It was around this time, and in this location, that the Visalia Ransacker case occurred. Many other burglaries happened at this time which might also be linked to the same perpetrator, but evidence from those days is unreliable. However, police may try to find links to around a hundred burglaries, and he is emerging as a suspect in the murder of Claude Snelling. Snelling was a teacher who was shot after trying to stop an intruder from kidnapping his daughter, who was just 16 at the time.

He then spent three years working for the police department in Auburn, California, but he was fired after being caught shoplifting. He had stolen a hammer and a can of dog repellant. Those who worked with him at that time describe a quiet man, a bit of a loner who liked his own company. But that does not make you a killer. Farrel Ward served with DeAngelo on the force.

'I've been thinking, but there's no indication whatsoever that anything was wrong. How could you just go out and kill somebody and go back to work? I don't understand that,' the 75-year-old former cop told reporters.

His current neighbors in Citrus Heights tell a similar story. The identify DeAngelo as a quiet man, more interested in keeping his lawn in perfect condition that causing any fuss in the neighborhood.

During the 1970s. DNA collection and profiling was just beginning to emerge as a tool for investigators of crime. As a serving policeman, DeAngelo would be familiar with police techniques, and how the emergence of DNA collection was beginning to lead to more secure convictions.

Following his departure from the police force, he took on a job in a grocery warehouse, where he worked for nearly thirty years. He also has a grown-up family.

Prior to the attacks beginning, Bonnie Ueltzen was engaged to marry DeAngelo. Then known as Bonnie Jean Colwell, the two fell in love in the early 1970s. They met when they were both students at Sierra College, which is based in Rocklin, California. But things did not work out, and some feel that this may have been a factor in the crimes that DeAngelo is alleged to have gone on to commit. One of his early rape victims reported to police that, following the attack on her, the perpetrator laid down on the bed next to her and began to cry. His words were:

'I hate you. I hate you. I hate you, Bonnie.'

What Next?

Joseph DeAngelo has so far been charged with the murder of Lyman and Charlene Smith. Their bodies were discovered by their twelve-year-old son. He was mowing the lawn and heard their alarm going off; he went to investigate when it was not turned off, and the discovery he made in that bloody bedroom was life changing.

It seems certain that further charges relating to the other killings and rapes will follow, with substantial numbers of burglary charges also perhaps to be added.

California needs though, to be careful and ensure that their inevitable and proper passions that have once more been distilled by his arrest do not cloud proper investigation and fair trial. Police are currently searching DeAngelo's home for trophies the killer took from the homes of his victims. That search continues, and like all aspects of this case, the investigation must be thorough, and any evidence found irrefutable. After all, if found guilty, DeAngelo faces the death penalty.

But the Golden State Killer case has already led to one devastating miscarriage of justice. Rhonda Wicht was just 24 when she was raped and both she and her four-year-old son were murdered in their home in 1978.

Craig Coley was 31, and Wicht's ex-boyfriend. He contacted police to find out more about their investigation, and within a day he had been arrested. Back in those days, guilt could be decided by the force on the basis of very little evidence, and that was what happened here.

Although the evidence linking him to the crime was sketchy and circumstantial, police did not bother with fingerprinting the crime scene and did not consider possibilities beyond the ex-boyfriend. A hung jury in the first trial favored conviction, but his second trial, which ended in January 1980, saw him convicted on two counts of murder. He was sentenced to life without parole.

But it was a former policeman from the Simi Valley region where Wicht had lived who began to realize that something was wrong. Michael Bender discovered Coley's file nearly ten years after his conviction and felt that something did not add up. He met with Coley and began to raise the possibility of wrongful conviction.

It was when DNA evidence proved that Coley had not been the attacker that he was exonerated.

It will be easy to assume that DeAngelo is the Golden State killer. The evidence reported so far seems strong, and the public want, need, an identifiable perpetrator. The police and local politicians might be keen to deliver one. The circumstantial evidence against DeAngelo is strong. He is the right age, lived in the right place and had a job that would make carrying out the crime easier. But many people are the right age and lived in the Sacramento region. Cold case investigator Paul Holes had concluded that there was no especial reason to feel that the killer was a member of the police or armed forces.

DeAngelo's name did not emerge in any way in the extensive investigations of Michelle McNamara and her co-citizen sleuths. Nor did it in the investigation carried out by police at the time, and Carol Daley's forty-year commitment to solving the case did not suggest DeAngelo.

The DNA evidence, from what we have heard from police so far, is strong. But the way it was collected is suspect. Evidence stored from the 1970s and early 80s may have been contaminated. Certainly, collection techniques are far less reliable than they are today.

His victims and the public at large now demand a proper, thorough investigation, where conclusions are reached after careful and full consideration. They seek a fair and open trial and if that delivers an unequivocal guilty verdict, then there is a small chance of a degree of closure for the many victims whose life has been ruined by the Golden State Killer.

But, in the interest of everybody affected by the sordid and evil acts begun four decades ago, California must be sure.

TED BUNDY

JOSEPH COLTON

Ted Bundy is one of the most prolific serial killers of the 20th century, having kidnapped, raped, and murdered at least 36 attractive young women between 1973 and 1978 in Colorado, Oregon, Utah, Florida, and Washington; however, many assert that this figure could be much higher. He had also kept some of his victims' body parts—including heads—as trophies in a utility shed behind his Utah home, as well having engaged in necrophilia with decomposing corpses which he would groom and apply makeup.

A master manipulator and classic antisocial personality, Bundy escaped custody twice; once from court during his first murder trial and the second time from the Garfield County Jail in Colorado by sawing a hole in his cell ceiling. He was placed on the FBI's Ten Most Wanted list and was later arrested in Florida in February 1978 after stealing a car. He was sentenced to death in 1979 for the murder of two Florida State University sorority sisters, and again in 1980 for another murder.

Very charismatic and handsome, Bundy exploited these characteristics heavily with his young female victims in an effort to earn their sympathy trust. He would often approach potential victims in public places, feigning injury or impersonating an authority figure before overpowering them—usually by hitting them in the head with a crowbar—taking them to secluded locations, and raping and murdering them. Sometimes he would simply break into young women's homes and bludgeon them while they slept.

Bundy was originally incarcerated for aggravated kidnapping and attempted assault in 1975 in Utah; however, his list of homicide victims continued to grow. He escaped from custody twice in Colorado and subsequently committed three more murders before finally being apprehended in Florida in 1978. Ted Bundy was sentenced to death and was executed in the electric chair at Raiford Prison in Starke, Florida, on 24 January 1989.

Early Life

Theodore Robert Bundy—originally Theodore Robert Cowell—was born on 24 November 1946 at the Elizabeth Lund Home for Unwed Mothers in Burlington, Vermont. The social stigma of being a single mother was great at that time so Bundy's mother, Louise Cowell, took her infant son to live with her parents—Samuel and Eleanor—in Philadelphia where young Ted took on the Cowell surname and was told that they were, in fact, his parents and that his mother was his sister. Eventually, Bundy discovered the truth and harbored lifelong resentment toward his mother for lying to him.

Bundy's paternity has never been definitively proven. His birth certificate lists his father as Lloyd Marshall, an Air Force veteran and salesman; however, Louise has claimed that she was "seduced by 'a sailor'" whose name "may have been Jack Worthington" but nobody by that name was ever found in Navy or merchant marines records. Compounding the problem is that Bundy's grandfather, Samuel Cowell, has been rumored to be his biological father; thus making Bundy the product of incest; however, again, there is no evidence of this.

In interviews, Bundy spoke highly of his grandparents, especially expressing a fondness for his grandfather even though other family members described Samuel as a tyrannical bully and bigot who beat his wife and dog, abused his daughters, harmed neighborhood cats, and would sometimes "speak aloud to unseen presences". Bundy's grandmother was timid and obedient and was treated for her depression with electroconvulsive therapy.

Bundy exhibited disturbing behavior from a young age. At the age of three, he was alleged to have surrounded his sleeping aunt, Julia, with household knives—blades pointed toward her—and smiled at her when she had awakened.

In 1950, when Bundy was only four, Louise changed both her and her son's surname to Nelson and moved them both to Tacoma, Washington, to live with cousins Jane and Alan Scott. In 1951, Louise met hospital cook Johnny Culpepper Bundy at a church singles night and they married later that year. Johnny formally adopted young Ted and he adopted the last name of Bundy. Even with efforts to include young Ted in family activities along with his four half-siblings—who he was often left to babysit—he always was distant. Later, Bundy would tell his girlfriend that Johnny wasn't his real dad, wasn't smart enough, and didn't make much money.

Bundy confessed that he "chose to be alone" as an adolescent and neither had any natural inclination to develop any close friendships nor knew what drove people to be friends in the first place. He would later say that he "hit a wall" and his inability to comprehend social behavior stunted his social development, rendering him required to adopt a façade of social activity. He was terribly shy, self-doubting, and uncomfortable in social situations and often teased for being different. Despite this, he was a good student at Woodrow Wilson High School, was active in a local Methodist church, and was even involved with a local Boy Scout troop.

Bundy would also admit—while on death row—that a part of him as a young child was "fascinated by images of sex and violence" and he called this part "the entity". He enjoyed reading crime books and detective magazines, particularly those that contained descriptions of sexual violence and pictures of dead bodies. Later, before his execution, he would admit that pornography was central in shaping who he was.

Throughout high school Bundy loved to ski and was very good at it; however, his pursuit of this hobby was usually accomplished with stolen equipment and forged lift tickets. He was also arrested on at least two occasions on suspicion of auto theft and burglary but when he turned 18 his juvenile record was expunged. Stealing, for Bundy, did not involve any guilt and, in fact, he had a sense of entitlement about the entire thing. He often said that the thrill of taking possession of something he wanted without remorse was exciting. Many speculate that his "taking" of his victims represented this same concept and provided him with the same rush. Compounding the problem was his sense of entitlement and cunning ability to lie about everything which demonstrates a common trait among psychopaths.

Bundy graduated high school in 1965 and was awarded a scholarship by the University of Puget Sound where he started that fall, taking courses in Oriental studies and psychology. After two semesters he transferred to the University of Washington in Seattle.

He obtained employment as a stock boy and bagger at a Safeway store on Queen Anne Hill, in addition to other odd jobs. As part of his psychology curricula, he would work as a night-shift volunteer at Seattle's Suicide Hot Line where he met and worked Ann Rule who would later become among the world's foremost true crime writers and who penned a biography about Bundy—that was also partly autobiographical about her working relationship with him—entitled *The Stranger Beside Me* (1980).

While in college, circa 1968, Bundy began a relationship with fellow student "Stephanie Brooks" (a pseudonym); however, after she graduated in 1968 and prepared to move back home to California she broke up with Bundy due to what she described as his lack of ambition and immaturity. Bundy was heartbroken after this and, interestingly, all of his victims bore some resemblance to Brooks; particularly the fact that Brooks and all of his victims had long dark hair which they wore parted down the middle.

Shortly thereafter, Bundy returned to Burlington—his birthplace—and learned the truth of his parentage. This discovery made him more dominant and focused.

He managed the Seattle office of Nelson Rockefeller's presidential campaign in 1968 and attended the 1968 Republican convention in Miami, Florida. He reenrolled at the University of Washington with a major in psychology. He became popular among his professors as he was an honor student and also began a relationship with Elizabeth Kloepfer in 1969. Kloepfer was a divorced secretary with a young daughter and the two dated for the next six years until he went to prison in 1976.

Bundy graduated in 1972 with a degree in psychology and went to work for the state Republican Party.

In the fall of 1973, Bundy enrolled in the University of Utah Law School but did poorly because of poor attendance and, consequently, dropped out the following spring.

While in California on a business trip in the summer of 1973, Bundy found his ex-girlfriend "Stephanie Brooks" and the change in his look and attitude was appealing to her. Bundy courted Brooks the rest of the year—while still involved with Kloepfer—and proposed to her, only to dump Brooks shortly after the new year, likely in retaliation for her breaking his heart years earlier. The breakup wreaked havoc on Bundy who became obsessed with her and this obsession "would span his lifetime and lead to a series of events that would shock the world".

Mere weeks later, Bundy began his first murderous rampage in Washington; however, many Bundy experts assert that he likely starting killing in his teens. One case involved eight-year-old Ann Marie Burr from Tacoma who disappeared from her home in 1961 when Bundy was 14. Burr's house was on Bundy's newspaper delivery route and her father was positive that he saw Bundy near a construction site ditch on the nearby University of Puget Sound campus the day his daughter vanished. Despite other potentially incriminating circumstantial evidence, Bundy remains merely a suspect due to a lack of consensus by law enforcement personnel as to whether they believe he actually did it or not. Bundy has always denied killing her.

Shortly before his execution, Bundy did, in fact, tell his attorney that his first attempt at kidnapping was in 1969 and his first "actual murder" occurred "sometime in 1972". While he was a suspect in the December 1973 murder of Kathy Devine in Washington, DNA analysis exonerated him and her true murderer was convicted in 2002. Bundy's earliest identified murders were committed in 1974 when he was 27.

Bundy was a handsome and charismatic guy, particularly to his young female victims and he exploited these characteristics fully. He was also an adept chameleon, able to blend in and feign belonging which increased his threat to the attractive brunette women he targeted as his victims. This charm and his adroitness at lying and manipulation made him extremely dangerous.

Known Murder Victims

Karen Sparks (often referred to as Joni Lenz), 18 (survived)

On 4 January 1974, 18-year-old Karen Sparks/Joni Lenz was found by her roommates when she didn't emerge from her bedroom that morning. They were not prepared for what horrific sights they saw. Sparks had been beaten badly and a bed rod ripped from the bed was "savagely rammed into her vagina". Sparks was transported to the hospital in a coma and suffered damages which continue to plague her.

However, she was one of the lucky few victims to survive an attack by Bundy.

Lynda Ann Healy, 21

A very accomplished and beautiful young woman, 21-year-old Lynda Healy announced ski conditions for all of the western Washington resorts on the radio. A senior at the University of Washington, she came from a good family, loved to sing, and was majoring in psychology. She shared a house with four other young women near the university. On 31 January, Healy and some friends went to a tavern and then home to bed. Her roommate in the next room never heard any sounds emanating from Healy's room that night.

The following morning when she didn't emerge from her bedroom after her alarm clock sounded at its usual 5:30 a.m. to go to work—and her job called looking for her—her roommate noticed that her bed was made in a peculiar way. Further inspection showed that the top sheet and a pillowcase were missing, a small bloodstain that was the same type as Lynda's was on the pillow and the bottom sheet, and a bloody nightgown was hanging in her closet. One of her outfits was missing. Also worrisome was that one of the doors was unlocked.

Initially, due to the absence of fingerprint, hair, or fiber evidence, police did not suspect foul play; however, later, they did come to realize that an intruder came in, removed Healy's nightgown and dressed her in another outfit, made the bed, wrapped her up, and took her out of the house.

Donna Gail Manson, 19

On 12 March, in Olympia, 19-year-old Evergreen State College student Donna Manson was kidnapped and murdered.

Susan Elaine Rancourt, 18

On 17 April, Susan Rancourt, 18, disappeared from the Central Washington State College campus in Ellensburg while walking across campus, alone, at night.

Later, two other female coeds would report meeting a good-looking man with his arm in a cast—one the night Rancourt disappeared and one three nights earlier—who asked for assistance with carrying books to his VW Beetle.

Roberta Kathleen "Kathy" Parks, 22

Kathy Parks, 22, was last seen on 6 May on the Oregon State University campus in Corvallis en route to meeting friends for coffee.

Brenda Carol Ball, 22

22-year-old Brenda Ball was last seen leaving the Flame Tavern in Burien, Oregon on 1 June.

Georgeann Hawkins, 18

In the early morning hours of 11 June, University of Washington student and a member of Kappa Alpha Theta Georgeann Hawkins, 18, left her boyfriend's dormitory en route to her sorority house through an alley. She was never seen again; however, witnesses later stated they had seen a man with a leg cast struggling to carry a briefcase in that area. Another female coed reported that he had asked her for help in carrying his briefcase to his VW Beetle.

Bundy later confessed to having lured Hawkins to his car, clubbed her with a tire iron he had hidden underneath his vehicle, and then took her elsewhere to rape and strangle her to death.

Janice Ann Ott, 23, and Denise Marie Naslund, 19

On 14 July, Janet Ott, 23, and Denise Naslund, 19, were abducted mere hours apart from Lake Sammamish State Park in Issaquah, Washington, in broad daylight. On that day, eight different witnesses reported seeing a handsome young man with his arm in a sling who called himself "Ted" and who asked several women for help unloading a sailboat from his VW Beetle. One witness said she walked with him for a ways but didn't see a sailboat and then declined to help him. Other witnesses stated that they saw the man approach Ott and she was observed walking away with him.

Naslund disappeared four hours later.

At this point, police in King County put up fliers with the suspected murderer's description all over the Seattle area. One of Bundy's psychology professors, former coworker Ann Rule, and Bundy's girlfriend Elizabeth Kloepfer reported him as a possible suspect. In fact, Kloepfer (who since changed her surname to Kendall and penned a book called *The Phantom Prince: My Life with Ted Bundy* in 1981) told the Seattle Police Department that her boyfriend "might be involved" in the recent Seattle murders. She called again later that autumn with more information and agreed to give them recent pictures of Bundy to be shown to witnesses; however, many of them could not positively identify him.

Ott's and Naslund's remains were found on 7 September off Interstate 90 near Issaquah, only one mile from the park where they were abducted. Near the women's remains was an extra femur and vertebrae which Bundy confessed before his execution belonged to Hawkins.

Between 1 March and 3 March 1975, the skulls and jawbones belonging to Healy, Rancourt, Parks, and Ball were found just east of Issaquah on Taylor Mountain. Bundy confessed in his death row interview that he kept the decapitated heads of these four victims in his apartment for some time and that he would revisit this dump site often to engage in sex with the corpses until decomposition became too great to continue. Bundy also admitted that he dumped Manson's body there as well—but burned her skull in his girlfriend's fireplace—however, no trace of her was ever recovered.

Other trophies discovered when Bundy's apartment was searched include photographs of his victims and a large bag of women's clothing.

Nancy Wilcox, 16

Bundy began the University of Utah Law School in the autumn of 1974. On 2 October 1974, 16-year-old Nancy Wilcox disappeared from Holladay, Utah. She was last seen in a VW Beetle.

Melissa Smith, 17

On 18 October, 17-year-old Melissa Smith—the daughter of Midvale, Utah's Police Chief Louis Smith—disappeared after leaving a pizza parlor. Nine days later she was found strangled, raped, and sodomized.

Laura Aime, 17

17-year-old Laura Aime disappeared from a Halloween party in Lehi, Utah. Her naked corpse was found on Thanksgiving Day by hikers near a river in the Wasatch Mountains. She had been beaten about the head and face with a crowbar and was raped and sodomized. The lack of blood at the crime scene indicated that she was likely killed elsewhere and dumped in this location. Police found no other physical evidence.

Carol DaRonch, 18 (survived)

On 8 November, 18-year-old Carol DaRonch was shopping at the Fashion Place Mall in Salt Lake City, Utah, and was approached by a man in the Sears parking lot who claimed to be a police officer named Officer Roseland. He told her that her car had been stolen and that he would take her to the police station to retrieve it. He took her to his VW Beetle and she became suspicious and asked him for identification. He quickly flashed a gold badge and she got in but refused his order to fasten her seat belt. After a short distance, Bundy pulled over and attempted to place handcuffs on DaRonch but only managed one wrist. He also attempted to hit her with a crowbar which she was able to catch before it hit her head. DaRonch fought back, kicking him in the groin, and as the car was speeding away she jumped out of it.

DaRonch flagged down another car and they took her to the police who confirmed there was no Officer Roseland. Police were able to obtain a description of the assailant and his car and a blood sample from DaRonch's coat. Type O; the same as Bundy's.

Debra Kent, 17

Mere hours after losing DaRonch Bundy abducted 17-year-old Debra "Debi" Kent from the parking lot of a school in Bountiful, Utah, as she was leaving a school play. She had told her parents she was going to pick up her brother at the bowling alley and she would be back to pick them up soon but never returned. She didn't even make it to her car which was still in the parking lot. Police found a small handcuff key in the parking lot and when they tried the key in the handcuffs DaRonch was wearing, it was a perfect fit.

A month later a man called the police and told them that he saw a tan VW Beetle speeding away from the high school parking lot the night Kent disappeared.

Shortly before he was to be executed, Bundy confessed that he dumped Kent's body near Fairview, Utah. After an intense search of the area, a human kneecap which was consistent with someone of Kent's age and size was found; however, DNA analysis was not conducted.

Caryn Campbell, 23

Bundy's first murder of 1975 occurred on 12 January. 23-year-old Michigan nurse Caryn Campbell disappeared between her hotel's lounge and her room while on a ski trip with her fiancé, Dr. Raymond Gadowski, and his two children, in Snowmass, Colorado. Frantic Gadowski called the police the next morning but a search proved futile.

Nearly a month later—and only a few short miles from where she went missing—a recreational worker discovered Campbell's nude body near the road. Animal damage to her body made it difficult to determine the exact cause of death; however, there was evidence of repeated, crushing blows to her head by a sharp instrument. Some of the blows were so violent that one of her teeth separated from the gums.

Julie Cunningham, 26

On 15 March, 26-year-old Vail ski instructor Julie Cunningham disappeared on her way to a nearby tavern. Bundy confessed in prison that he used his crutches ploy to approach Cunningham to ask for her help carrying ski boots to his car before he clubbed her with his crowbar, handcuffed her, and took her to a secluded location where strangled her.

Denise Oliverson, 25

25-year-old Denise Oliverson vanished in Grand Junction on 6 April while riding her bicycle to visit her parents.

Lynette Culver, 13

13-year-old Lynette Culver was abducted from her school playground at Alameda Junior High School in Pocatello, Idaho.

Susan Curtis, 15

Once Bundy returned to Utah, 15-year-old Susan Curtis vanished on 28 June while walking alone to the Brigham Young University dormitories during a youth conference she was attending. Bundy confessed to her murder minutes before his execution.

The bodies of Cunningham, Oliverson, Culver, and Curtis have never been found.

First Arrest, Trial, and Escapes

Bundy was first arrested on 16 August 1975 in Salt Lake City for failure to stop his vehicle for police. A search of his car unearthed a crowbar, handcuffs, ski mask, trash bags, an icepick, and other items the officer thought were burglary tools. The always calm and collected Bundy explained reasons why he had the items such as that he used the mask for skiing and had found the handcuffs in a dumpster; however, Detective Jerry Thompson connected Bundy and his Volkswagen to the DaRonch kidnapping and other missing girls and searched his apartment.

The search yielded a brochure of Colorado ski resorts with a checkmark by where Campbell had disappeared. Bundy was brought in for a lineup before DaRonch and other witnesses at the time DaRonch was kidnapped and they all identified him as Officer Roseland, as well as the man lurking about on the night Debbie Kent vanished.

After a week-long trial, Bundy was convicted on 1 March 1976 of kidnapping DaRonch and was sentenced to 15 years in Utah State Prison. Bundy was then extradited to Colorado to stand trial for murder.

He was able to escape custody twice before his eventual final arrest in Florida. The first escape occurred on 7 June 1977, when he was transported from the Garfield County Jail in Glenwood Springs, Colorado, to Pitkin County Courthouse in Aspen for his preliminary hearing. As he was serving as his own attorney, the judge excused him from being handcuffed and shackled. During a recess Bundy asked if he could research his case in the courthouse's law library. Hiding behind a bookcase he jumped from a second-story window, spraining his ankle when he landed. After shedding his suit, he simply walked through the town of Aspen as roadblocks were being erected before hiking southward on Aspen Mountain.

Near its summit he burglarized a cabin and stole clothing, food, and a rifle before heading toward Crested Butte; however, Bundy became lost and ended up wandering aimlessly for two days before breaking into a camping trailer on Maroon Lake where he took more food and a parka. Bundy then walked back toward Aspen and stole a car parked at the Aspen Golf Course. Two police officers noticed him weaving in traffic and pulled over the six-day fugitive. In the car were maps of the mountains around Aspen that the prosecutor was using to demonstrate where victim Caryn Campbell's body was found. As Bundy was his own attorney, he had the right of discovery to this evidence, thus demonstrating that he had planned his escape.

Bundy's second escape occurred on 30 December 1977, after having his motion for a change of venue to Denver accepted but with the venue being Colorado Springs instead; a city that had historically been hostile to murder suspects. He had managed to acquire the jail's floor plan and a hacksaw blade from other inmates, as well as $500 in cash smuggled in over a six-month period by visitors—particularly one Carole Ann Boone. In the evening while other inmates were showering, Bundy sawed a one-foot-square hole in his cell's ceiling—behind the steel bars—and was able to fit through it into the crawlspace above after losing 35 pounds. Prior to his actual escape, Bundy "practiced" and multiple reports of possible movement in the ceiling's crawlspace were, curiously, never investigated.

On the night of his escape, Bundy piled files and books under his covers in his bunk to look like his sleeping body, climbed into the crawlspace, broke through the jail's ceiling which, incidentally, was the chief jailer's apartment who just happened to be out for the evening with his wife. Bundy stole some street clothes and casually sauntered out the front door.

Bundy stole a car and drove east; however, the car broke down on Colorado's Interstate 70. A passing motorist gave him a ride into Vail where he caught a bus to Denver and then took a flight to Chicago, Illinois. From there he took an Amtrak train to Ann Arbor, Michigan.

His escape was discovered over 17 hours after the fact at noon on New Year's Eve.

Lisa Levy, 20, Margaret Bowman, 21, Karen Chandler (survived), Kathy Kleiner Deshields (survived)

On 15 January 1978—after Bundy had escaped from jail in Colorado, he traveled to Tallahassee, Florida, and attacked Chi Omega sorority sisters at Florida State University. At approximately 3:00 a.m. he entered the sorority house where he raped and strangled 20-year-old Lisa Levy to death; bludgeoned 21-year-old Margaret Bowman to death; and also bludgeoned Karen Chandler and Kathy Kleiner—both of whom survived.

The entire rampage took only 30 minutes.

Cheryl Thomas (survived)

That same morning, a mere eight blocks from the Chi Omega sorority house, Bundy attacked Cheryl Thomas in her bed and bludgeoned her with a wooden club, severely injuring her.

Kimberly Leach, 12

On 9 February, Bundy kidnapped 12-year-old Kimberly Leach from her junior high school in Lake City, Florida. Her raped, murdered, and dumped body was found in Suwannee River State Park underneath a small pig shed.

Bundy then stole another VW Beetle and left Tallahassee, traveling west across the Florida panhandle.

Florida Arrest

On 15 February 1978 shortly after 1:00 a.m., Bundy was stopped by Pensacola police officer David Lee who learned that the vehicle was stolen. After a brief scuffle, Lee had subdued and restrained Bundy and then took him to jail. During the transport, Bundy allegedly told Lee that he wished the officer would have killed him. Once his identity was confirmed, Bundy was transported to Tallahassee and charged with the Tallahassee and Lake City murders.

Florida Trials and Convictions

Among the most damning evidence during Bundy's June 1979 Chi Omega murder trial were bite marks found on Lisa Levy's left buttock which matched a plaster cast taken from Bundy's mouth. Additionally, Chi Omega sister Nita Neary was returning home late that night and saw Bundy as he left. She was able to identify him in court.

Bundy was convicted on all counts and sentenced to death.

In 1980, Bundy stood trial for the Kimberly Leach murder. Again, he was convicted, this time based upon fiber evidence and an eyewitness who saw him leading Leach away from the school. Bundy was, again, sentenced to death.

After his sentences he sought a stay of execution or commutation of his death sentences to life imprisonment by having one of his legal advocates contact his victims' families to ask them to ask for mercy in order to find out where their loved ones' remains were. This ploy for more time failed.

Execution

Bundy ultimately met his demise in Raiford Prison's electric chair on 24 January 1989.

Shortly before his widely-publicized execution, Bundy confessed to 36 murders in seven states; however, many believe that the total number is much higher. Also before his execution, Bundy contacted Dr. James Dobson, psychologist and founder of the Christian evangelical organization Focus on the Family, and agreed to a television interview the day before his execution. In it, Bundy described the influence of pornography on his behavior. While not expressly blaming pornography for his behavior, Bundy did say that pornographic materials shaped and molded his behavior and he would gradually need more violent, graphic, and explicit material to achieve the same "high"; not unlike a drug addict. He claimed that while murdering he was "possessed by 'something ... awful and alien'" and the brutal urge was indescribable. He also claimed that alcohol helped remove the initial boundary for him to commit his first murder. Bundy also admitted that although he believed he deserved the death penalty, he didn't want to die.

Even today, Bundy remains a suspect in a number of open homicide cases and is likely responsible for other victims who will never be identified. In 1987 he confided to Keppel that there were some murders that he would "never talk about" because they were committed too close to home, involved victims who were very young, or were too close to family. Said victims include the aforementioned Ann Marie Burr who Bundy repeatedly denied having murdered; however, Keppel noticed that Burr fits all three of Bundy's "no discussion" categories. In 2011, forensic testing of material from the Burr crime scene did not have enough intact DNA sequences to compare to Bundy's.

Additional potential victims include flight attendants Lisa E. Wick and Lonnie Trumbull, both 20, who were bludgeoned with a piece of wood while asleep in their Seattle home on 23 June 1966 that was very near the Safeway store where Bundy worked at the time, and where the victims regularly shopped. Trumbull did not make it and Wick suffered permanent memory loss.

On 30 May 1969 college friends Susan Davis and Elizabeth Perry, both 19, who were on vacation in Atlantic City, New Jersey—just 60 miles south of Philadelphia—were found stabbed to death in the woods three days later.

On 19 July 1971, 24-year-old elementary school teacher and motel maid Rita Curran was murdered in her basement apartment in Burlington, Vermont. She had been bludgeoned, raped, and strangled. The motel where she worked part-time was adjacent to the Elizabeth Lund Home where Bundy was born and certain similarities to his other crime scenes made Bundy a suspect.

21-year-old Joyce LePage was last seen alive on 22 July 1971 on the Washington State University campus. Nine months later her skeleton was found wrapped in military blankets, carpeting, and rope, at the bottom of a Pullman, Washington, ravine.

On 29 June 1973, 17-year-old Rita Lorraine Jolly disappeared from West Linn, Oregon while 24-year-old Vicki Lynn Hollar disappeared from Eugene, Oregon, on 20 August of that same year. Bundy had confessed to two Oregon homicides but did not identify the victims.

Brenda Joy Baker, 14, was last seen hitchhiking near Puyallup, Washington on 27 May 1974 and her body would be discovered a month later in Millersylvania State Park.

19-year-old Wisconsin native Sandra Jean Weaver who had been living in Tooele, Utah, was last seen on 1 July 1974 in Salt Lake City. Her nude body was found the following day in Grand Junction, Colorado.

20-year-old Carol Valenzuela was last seen hitchhiking near Vancouver, Washington, on 2 August 1974 and her remains were found two months later in a shallow grave south of Olympia; along with the remains of another female who was later identified as 17-year-old Martha Morrison who was last seen in Eugene, Oregon, on 1 September 1974. During this time, Bundy drove from Seattle to Salt Lake City and could have conceivably passed through both towns; however, there is no definitive evidence.

Bundy is also a suspect in Melanie Suzanne Cooley's disappearance on 15 April 1975 after leaving Nederland High School in Nederland, Colorado. Her beaten and strangled corpse was discovered on 2 May by road maintenance workers nearby in Coal Creek Canyon. Whereas gas receipts place Bundy in Golden that day—not far from Nederland—the Jefferson County Sheriff's Office has classified her murder as a cold case.

On 1 July 1975, Shelly Kay Robertson, 24, failed to show up for work in Golden, Colorado, and her nude, decomposed corpse was found in August inside of a mine on Berthoud Pass near Winter Park. While gas station receipts place Bundy in the area, there is no direct evidence as to his complicity.

23-year-old Nancy Perry Baird disappeared from the Farmington, Utah, service station where she worked on 4 July 1975. She officially remains a missing person and Bundy has repeatedly denied involvement.

Finally, 17-year-old Debbie Smith was last seen in February 1976 in Salt Lake City before the DaRonch trial. Her body was found near the airport on 1 April 1976.

Aftermath

During the Kimberly Leach trial, Bundy married Carole Ann Boone. He took advantage of an existing Florida statute in which a marriage declaration in court in front of a judge constituted a legal marriage. Thus, Bundy called Boone as a character witness and married her while she was on the witness stand. After numerous conjugal visits, Boone gave birth to a daughter in October 1982. She returned to Washington in 1986 with her daughter after divorcing him and never returned.

Ann Rule described Bundy as "... a sadistic sociopath who took pleasure from another human's pain and the control he had over his victims, to the point of death, and even after." He once referred to himself as "the most cold-hearted son of a bitch you'll ever meet" and one of his defense attorneys, Polly Nelson, said that Bundy "was the very definition of heartless evil." At one point, Bundy said, "We serial killers are your sons, we are your husbands, we are everywhere. And there will be more of your children dead tomorrow."

Bundy contacted Robert Keppel—the detective who helped put him in prison—while on death row to assist him with the "Green River Killer" investigation at the time. With Bundy's assistance, Keppel was able to understand the inner workings of the mind of a serial killer and was, subsequently, able to identify and apprehend Gary Ridgway in November 2001.

Ted Bundy has been the subject of three television movies and one feature film. The two-part film entitled *The Deliberate Stranger* aired on NBC in 1986, starring Mark Harmon as Bundy. *Ted Bundy* (2002) starred Michael Reilly Burke as Bundy and was directed by Matthew Bright. In 2003 the USA

Network aired Ann Rule's *The Stranger Beside Me* that starred Billy Campbell as Bundy and Barbara Hershey as Rule. Finally, the A&E network produced an adaptation of detective Robert Keppel's book *The Riverman* in 2004, starring Cary Elwes as Bundy and Bruce Greenwood as Keppel.

THE TRAILSIDE KILLER

39

David Carpenter ("Trailside Killer")

David Carpenter, also known as the Trailside Killer, stalked, sexually assaulted, and murdered mostly women on hiking trails near San Francisco, California, with a few victims in Santa Cruz, California. Most of his victims were shot in the head, execution-style, while a couple of them were stabbed to death. Carpenter's reign of terror lasted from 1979 into 1981 when he was subsequently arrested, tried, and convicted of death.

One of his victims, Stephen Haertle, survived being shot multiple times by Carpenter—even though his girlfriend Ellen Hansen was killed—and was able to give police a description of his assailant. Additional witness testimony placed a small red foreign car in the area. Carpenter matched the composite drawn from Haertle's description and he also owned a car that matched the description of the one on the scene at the time of Hansen's and Haertle's attack.

Carpenter was convicted in two separate trials; one in Los Angeles and one in San Diego. Both trials were relocated due to defense attorneys' requests for changes of venue.

He was ultimately sentenced to death and is currently on San Quentin's death row. Carpenter is 85 years of age.

Early Life

David Joseph Carpenter was born on 6 May 1930 in San Francisco—a place that would later become his hunting grounds. As a child, he was physically abused and neglected by his alcoholic father while his near-blind mother was overly domineering. By the time he was seven years old, his stutter was so bad that he couldn't function in any social situation. Many experts assert that his stuttering was likely a result of stress, self-perceived inadequacy, and not feeling safe as a child. Consequently he was ridiculed which made him overly reclusive. Instead of therapy he was forced to take ballet and piano lessons.

To relieve his frustrations, Carpenter suffered from a bedwetting problem and also tortured animals; thus fulfilling two of the three prongs of the classic serial killer triad, with the other being a preoccupation with setting fires.

From a young age he also had an insatiable sex drive and would look for opportunities to express this. At the age of 17 Carpenter was incarcerated for molesting two of his young cousins. He served a year in the custody of the California Youth Authority and apparently learned nothing because after his release he was even more predatory; offending until he got married in 1955.

Carpenter worked a number of jobs, including as a cruise ship's purser, a salesman, and a printer.

Carpenter and his wife had three children and Carpenter's demanding libido got to be too much for her. Eventually his wife was not enough to satisfy him. In addition to his violent rages he would prowl around, looking for other women. When his drive became so desperate, he resorted to violence.

By serial killer standards, Carpenter was a late bloomer. His first serious violent offense occurred in 1960 when he was arrested and incarcerated for attempted murder for attacking a woman with a hammer and knife. He had befriended this woman and invited her over to meet his wife and family. One day he picked her up for work but instead of driving her there he drove to a wooded area near the Presidio and then pretended to be lost. At some point he grabbed her, straddled her, and tied her up with a clothesline. He then threatened her with a knife, forcing her to be still and telling her that he had a "funny quirk" that needed to be satisfied. When she resisted he struck her multiple times with a hammer. Her cries for help alerted a nearby military patrol officer who, essentially, saved her life. When commanded to stop, Carpenter shot at the officer and was met with return gunfire which wounded Carpenter. He was then arrested. The victim survived. The victim described his speech to investigators as slow and deliberate, thus suggesting that when Carpenter feels as though he is in charge of a situation and asserting himself then he loses his stutter.

While initially sentenced to 14 years, Carpenter served just nine before being released in 1969. Tired of his sexual demands and temper—and having just given birth to their third child—his wife divorced him. When questioned about what caused the divorce Carpenter's story would change, thus indicating that he learned to tell people what he thought they wanted to hear.

Carpenter was remarried quickly after his release and in less than a year this marriage failed as he was back to his old tricks. He once tried to rape a woman by hitting her car to force her out of it. As she struggled with him he stabbed her but she managed to get back into her car and get help.

At this point there is little doubt that Carpenter wanted to rape again but not return to prison so he was prepared to eliminate any witnesses.

He was rearrested on 3 February 1970, in Modesto, California, on kidnapping and robbery charges. Before being transferred to prison, however, he and four other inmates escaped from the Calaveras County Jail. After recapture by the Federal Bureau of Investigation, Carpenter was incarcerated for seven years on the kidnapping and robbery charges, with two more for violating parole. He served his time and was then paroled in May 1979, without being listed as a sex offender which he should have been. In August of that year he murdered his first of many victims.

Carpenter found a job at a photo print shop in San Francisco after he left prison and by all measures appeared to be on the right path to becoming a productive and law-abiding citizen.

The Crimes

Edda Kane

44-year-old married bank executive Edda Kane disappeared from Mount Tamalpais Park near San Francisco Bay on 19 August 1979, while hiking in the part of the park nicknamed "the Sleeping Lady" to revel in the glorious view of the Golden Gate Bridge. As she enjoyed an athletic lifestyle and could not find someone to accompany her on her hike that day, she decided to go out alone. When she did not return home that day her husband called the police who sent out a search team with dogs in case she had fallen and required assistance.

Kane's vehicle was in the parking lot where she left it but there were no signs of the missing woman.

She was later found off Rock Spring Trail on 20 August 1979, naked and shot to death. Forensic experts surmised that she had been attacked from behind and then shot execution-style with a bullet in the back of the head based upon the position of her body on its knees with her face in the dirt. $10 was missing from her wallet, along with some credit cards. The attacker took her glasses but left her jewelry.

This was the first murder on Mount Tamalpais.

Kane's autopsy demonstrated that she had been shot once in the back of the head with a .44 caliber gun. As she had not been raped, police were dumbfounded as to the motive for the attack. Nobody who knew the victim could think of anyone who would want to do her any harm and the lack of evidence did not permit police to fully investigate her death. After a short time her murder became an unsolved isolated homicide and things returned to normal until the following spring.

Barbara Schwartz

On 7 March 1980, 23-year-old baker Barbara Schwartz had gone hiking in Mount Tamalpais State Park with her dog and had never returned.

She was found on a narrow unpaved trail, stabbed to death in the chest. A witness who had watched the entire crime ran for help and, thus, led the rangers to the crime scene. The witness was hiking in the area when she saw through the trees a thin, athletic man, about 25 years of age approach Schwartz whose dog was barking. She said the assailant "had a hawk nose and dark hair, and he wore hiking boots." The witness then stated that the man and victim struggled for nearly a minute and then he left as Schwartz fell to the ground which was when she left to seek help. Unfortunately, the witness' description of the assailant was "wildly erroneous in every respect" and she, in fact, later admitted this herself. Consequently, investigators were misled, thus delaying the search for the actual culprit.

Other witnesses said they had seen a lone male in his 40s, wearing glasses, and clad in a raincoat despite the fact that it wasn't raining that day. This man was most likely Schwartz's killer.

The bifocals found near Schwartz's body turned out to be prison-issued so investigators began to look at recently-released convicts, particularly those with a record of sex crimes who bore some resemblance to the witness description of the assailant. The San Francisco office of the FBI assisted with the investigation but to no avail.

Interestingly, however, police in another jurisdiction did question a man who claimed to have been wounded in a convenience store attack; however, these officers did not have access to the Marin County all-points bulletin and, therefore, were unable to make a possible connection that this quiet man may have been responsible for Schwartz's murder. The next day the same wounded man visited an optometrist—Schwartz's doctor, in fact—to get a new pair of glasses. The previous day the police had questioned the doctor about Schwartz's prescription; however, he had no knowledge of the eyeglasses found at the scene of the crime. If he had then he might have recognized the "unique prescription" his new patient had.

During Schwartz's autopsy, the pathologist counted 12 separate stab wounds in her chest, likely made with a ten-inch knife. Several days later, some kids found a blood-crusted boning knife near the crime scene which was determined to have been purchased at a large chain grocery store. A television reporter had subsequently handled the knife, thus obliterating any fingerprints which might have been left by the murderer. Forensic evidence suggested that she, too, had been in a kneeling position when she died.

Anne Alderson

On 15 October 1980, 26-year-old former Peace Corps volunteer Anne Alderson entered the park to go for a jog and to demonstrate that the park was, for the most part, safe. Many witnesses saw her and the park's caretaker even remembered her sitting alone in the 5,000-seat amphitheater to watch the sunset. Earlier that day some of the same witnesses reported seeing a lone male around 50 years of age in the park "just standing around."

She was found the next day with a .38 caliber bullet in her head. This crime scene was different from the others in that Alderson was raped, then permitted to get dressed before being murdered. She was found propped, face up, against a rock with her right earring missing. Investigators believed that "her twisted arrangement" indicated that she may have been forced to kneel as well before being shot.

Mark McDermand—A Red Herring

Police thought they had the person responsible for her death when they investigated a double homicide on 16 October 1980, near Mount Tamalpais in Mill Valley. Mark McDermand, 35, and his brother, Edwin, 40, both lived with their mother, Helen, 75. At approximately 8:30 p.m. deputies responded to a call by a concerned friend. After forcing their way into the home, deputies found the body of a man lying in a hallway who was identified as Edwin. He had been shot in the head and chest. In a locked bedroom deputies found the deceased body of Helen, lying on the bed and covered by a blanket. She had a single bullet hole behind her left ear. Eight spent .22 caliber casings were found near the bodies.

Deputies found a small padlocked door that led to the basement. They discovered a note tacked to the inside of the door addressed to "Shitheels" that said that by the time the note and bodies were discovered it would be "way too late" and that the perpetrator would be found either "on the news or on a 'slab'". The note was signed "Mr. Hate."

Inside the room were spent .38 caliber casings, three .22 caliber bullets, and ankle holsters for a pistol and a knife. This smelly basement room had been Mark McDermand's bedroom and became the prime suspect.

The coroner said that the bodies had been dead for three or four days.

A few days later, the local newspaper and the Marin County Sheriff's Department received letters from an individual claiming responsibility for the double homicide and a handwriting expert stated that the same person who wrote the note at the McDermand's house also wrote these letters. In these letters, the writer stated that he would not be captured alive so on 24 October detectives devised a plan to lure him by running an ad directed at him with a phone number that said that if he surrendered he would be treated fairly.

McDermand called the number that evening and said that he was considering surrendering but that "he had some things to do first." He called again two days later with details about the murders; saying that he tried to kill his mother and brother quickly but miscalculated with Edwin, hence the multiple gunshot wounds. He said that he had to "stop Edwin from hurting others" and that he would turn himself in the next day.

When McDermand approached the police he was wearing a belt with a .38 caliber revolver and also had a set of thumb cuffs and three speed loaders. In his vehicle was a 12-gauge shotgun, a .22 caliber pistol, ammunition, a metal box containing several hypodermic syringes, and some insulin as McDermand was diabetic.

He told police that his brother was schizophrenic and had been deteriorating quickly so he borrowed the guns and then prepared to go on the run after the deed was done. McDermand said that he acted out of diminished capacity and that he, too, was schizophrenic and couldn't remember the murders or when he did he told several different stories.

Nevertheless, the jury found McDermand guilty of two counts of first-degree murder and he received the death penalty.

At the end of it all, investigators resolved his potential part in the trailside murders as none of his firearms matched the bullets found in the victims on Mount Tampalpais. That and the fact that the murders continued.

Shauna May

On 27 November 1980 25-year-old Shauna May disappeared from Point Reyes National Seashore Park while hiking. She was supposed to meet friends the following day to do more hiking. They had selected this area because it was several miles north of San Francisco and had not had the dubious distinction of having had a murder occur there recently. When she failed to show up, her friends alerted park officials.

Two days later her body was found by hikers who had seen her foot protruding from a shallow grave. She had been strangled with picture frame wire, shot three times in the head, and shoved into a shallow trench. She had also been raped.

Her body was found in close proximity to Diane O'Connell.

Diane O'Connell

The body of 22-year-old Diane O'Connell was found the same day and near May's body. She had disappeared a month earlier from the same area while hiking with friends as well and her body was rather decomposed. She had been raped, strangled with wire, and shot once in the head.

It was initially believed that the two women perhaps knew each other and were killed at around the same time as another hiker reported hearing four gunshots in that area of the park during the mid-afternoon.

The two women were laying together, face down. Their collective clothing was piled atop a backpack. A pair of underwear was stuffed into O'Connell's mouth. After investigating, it was determined that the two women did not know each other.

Richard Stowers and Cynthia Moreland

As if finding two bodies wasn't bad enough, police also discovered the bodies of 19-year-old Richard Towers and his girlfriend, 18-year-old Cynthia Moreland on the same day as May's and O'Connell's. The couple had been missing since 11 October, having last been seen by friends who they told that they were going to go hiking in the park. In fact, Stowers was in the Coast Guard and was reported as being AWOL.

Both victims had been murdered execution-style with bullets to the head.

An autopsy placed their time of death mere days before Alderson's, thus suggesting that there were two murderers or that a single killer had gone hunting for victims in two different areas. When ballistics determined that the bullet from Alderson's head matched those in both Stowers and Moreland, authorities knew there was just one single deadly predator.

Visitors were told not to go hiking alone; however, being together did not save Stowers and Moreland. Those who typically frequented the parks stayed away or went elsewhere until the murderer was caught.

Needless to say, the media frenzy that ensued wreaked panic throughout the area.

Was David Carpenter the Elusive Zodiac Killer?

Between December 1968 and July 1969 a man shot two couples on two separate occasions in Vallejo, California and then taunted detectives with phone calls claiming responsibility. One of the victims survived and was able to give police a description. Soon thereafter, editors of three San Francisco newspapers each received part of a strange letter also claiming to be from the killer. His message "consisted of a printed cryptogram composed of symbols and signed with a crossed-circle symbol" and all three of the letters had to be put together to decipher it. A local teacher was able to crack the code which stated that the killer enjoyed killing and it was his intention to continue doing so. He signed his letter "the Zodiac."

On 27 September 1969, while 20-year-old Bryan Hartnell and 22-year-old Cecelia Ann Shepard were picnicking at Lake Berryessa, a man in a black executioner's hood approached them. He stabbed Shepard ten times—five in the front and five in the back—and Hartnell six times in the back. He then called the police to report it.

Two weeks later the killer struck again, killing cab driver Paul Stine. The *San Francisco Chronicle* received a letter soon after accompanied by a torn piece of the shirt Stine was wearing at the time of his death. Investigators developed a number of suspects but none checked out. This serial killer was very clever and turned his escapades into multilayered games before he withdraw and maintained a low profile. This was quite disturbing for investigators who never knew when or where he would resurface.

In 1980, former FBI profiler John Douglas—who had been on the Zodiac case since it began—assisted sex crimes expert Special Agent Roy Hazelwood and San Francisco police to help create a profile of the Trailside Killer.

After examining the crime scene data and photos, Douglas concluded that the killer would be a local man who was shy, reclusive, and may have a speech impediment. Douglas also added that the murderer was likely socially awkward, white, intelligent, blue collar, and had spent time incarcerated. He was presumed to choose his victims out of opportunity rather than hunting the same type of victim. His modus operandi (MO) was to approach from behind and overwhelm his victim—"like a spider waiting for a bug to fly into his web." Douglas added that the killer would also have at least two of three specific background indicators common to many serial killers: bedwetting, fire-starting, and cruelty to animals. Finally, Douglas had said while the suspect likely committed rape in his past he had not killed anyone before his current murderous rampage. When questioned about the very specific speech impediment predictor, Douglas said that the secluded killing areas and method of approach indicated some type of shyness and/or shame and he believed it was due to some physical malady that really bothered the killer. Therefore, he attacked in the way he did to compensate for his handicap. While being very detailed, however, police still didn't have any potential suspects.

After Douglas returned to Quantico the Trailside Killer struck again.

Carpenter was ultimately cleared of any involvement with the Zodiac murders through fingerprint and handwriting analysis.

Ellen Hansen

On 29 March 1981, University of California at Davis undergraduate students Ellen Hansen and her boyfriend Stephen Haertle were ambushed in Henry Cowell State Park near Santa Cruz; another town that experienced a spate of murders during the early 1970s committed by Edmund Kemper, John Linley Frazier, and Herbert Mullin—all of whom were safely incarcerated at that time.

Carpenter approached the couple with a pistol in his hand and threatened the pair, insisting that Hansen permit him to rape her. Of course she refused, telling him off. Carpenter then opened fire, shooting Hansen point blank in the head twice and once in the shoulder. The assailant then shot Haertle and left him for dead. Haertle crawled for help despite wounds that ripped through his neck, a hand, and one eye. He proved instrumental in providing police with a partial description of the murderer: near 50, balding, approximately five-foot-ten to six-feet tall and approximately 170 pounds, with crooked yellow teeth, wearing dark glasses as well as a gold jacket with lettering on the back and a baseball cap. Haertle also remembered that the assailant had spoken in "quick, commanding sentences." This description differed considerably from the description Jun of the Marin County killer; however, the MO was the same.

Other hikers reported that they had seen a man matching the description of the gunman in a red, late model, foreign car, running through the park after the gunshots had been fired.

Investigators were also able to lift some good shoeprint impressions to compare to a suspect when they got one.

Authorities released a composite drawing based upon Haertle's and other witness' descriptions in a number of newspapers to both alert people and hopefully get some leads. Four days later a woman called to describe a man she had met 26 years earlier on a cruise to Japan. She said that the purser on the cruise was a young man named David Carpenter who had been bothering her and her daughter with inappropriate behavior. She also recalled that he stuttered.

Presumably reading the paper and staying abreast with detectives' search for the Trailside Killer, Carpenter decided to grow a beard.

He then decided to kill much closer to home, enabling police to catch him.

Heather Scaggs

On 1 May 1981 police caught a break; however, it would come with another victim. On that day, 20-year-old Heather Scaggs disappeared on her way en route to buy a car with help from a coworker, one David Carpenter; they both worked at Econo Quick Print. She had told her boyfriend, Dan Pingle, that Carpenter "made a special point" of asking her to come alone when she came by to get the car and that his friend was selling it and Carpenter was going to help her purchase it. It was Pingle who informed police that she was missing. Luckily Scaggs had left Carpenter's address and phone number with him.

Scaggs' decomposing body was found on 24 May 1981 in Big Basin Redwood State Park, north of San Francisco. Ballistics from recovered bullets proved that she had been murdered with the same pistol used on Haertle and Hansen. She had also been raped and the DNA from the semen inside of her matched Carpenter.

Anna Menjivas

On 16 June 1981 a jaw bone later identified as belonging to Anna Menjivas was found by rock climbers in Castle Rock State Park. She had been missing since 28 December 1980 and was 17 years old at the time of her disappearance.

She had worked part-time at the bank where Carpenter was a client and he often struck up conversation with her. Many believed that he only came into the bank to talk to her. Because the cause of death could not be established and there was scant evidence against him, he was not charged for her murder even though authorities were certain that he had killed her. Her name was added to the list of Carpenter's victims to bring his total to ten murders.

Investigation and Arrest

When police went to Carpenter's house to question him, they couldn't help but notice that Carpenter looked quite like the man in the composite sketch and that he had a shiny red Fiat.

Police discovered that Carpenter had not shown up on any released inmates' records where they initially searched due to a technicality: that he had been released by the state of California to serve a federal sentence and, while out on parole, was technically in federal custody. This issue resulted in the delay and subsequent difficulty in identifying him. That he was a habitual sex offender was another important factor not fully documented in his records.

The police department and FBI set up a surveillance van outside the house at 36 Sussex Street in San Francisco where Carpenter lived with his aging parents and also followed him on his errands, especially when he associated with other known criminals. They approached Carpenter who was walking down the street one day with a shopping bag in his hand to apprehend him. Initially confused, Carpenter then asked for a lawyer; at this point he was told that he was under arrest, to which he, strangely, begged, "Please don't hurt me."

Officers executed a search warrant on Carpenters home and car and found books about local hiking trails and over 60 maps. They talked to Carpenter's former fiancée who told them that he claimed that the gold jacket he once owned was stolen around the time of the Hansen murder; thus circumstantially placing him at the scene where Haertle and Hansen were shot. Further, Carpenter's car matched the one described by the surviving victim and several witnesses, he had the same optometrist as another victim, he had the right distinctive type of clothing, he had a record for violent sex offenses, he suffered from explosive rage and tried to change his appearance with different glasses and facial hair, and he matched many descriptions witnesses gave as the man who had been seen in the area of multiple attacks.

Haertle picked Carpenter's mugshot as the man who shot him and killed his girlfriend. Out of seven more witnesses present at a lineup, six picked him out although not all of them were sure. Police also conducted a car lineup with witnesses identifying Carpenter's Fiat.

He was formally charged with Hansen's murder and Haertle's attempted murder. At his arraignment Carpenter stuttered so badly that he had a difficult time answering the judges questions.

Police were never able to recover the .45 caliber gun that was used in several of his murders; however, a .38 caliber gun that Carpenter had sold to another man, who was on trial for robbery and gladly relinquished it to authorities, was later proven to be the firearm used in the last two murders.

Trial and Conviction

Carpenter's defense attorneys requested a change of venue due to the publicity surrounding his ten murders. However, if attorneys had thought it would make a difference they were mistaken. A change of venue would do nothing to eliminate the incriminating evidence police had against Carpenter. In April 1984, his Los Angeles trial began and on 6 July 1984, Carpenter was convicted of the Santa Cruz murders of Heather Scaggs and Ellen Hansen, and the attempted murder of Stephen Haertle thanks to the damning evidence that his gun was the one responsible for their deaths. A second jury sentenced Carpenter to die in San Quentin's gas chamber based upon three special circumstances that warranted the death penalty: that he had committed multiple murders; that he had murdered during commission of rape; and that he had lain in wait for his victims. Judge Dion Morrow told the court that, "The defendant's entire life has been a continuous expression of violence and force almost beyond exception. I must conclude with the prosecution that if ever there was a case appropriate for the death penalty, this is it."

Carpenter's second trial began on 5 January 1988 in San Diego. On 10 May 1988, a San Diego jury found Carpenter guilty for five murders. Carpenter was also found guilty of two counts of rape and one count of attempted rape. This trial was different in that Carpenter himself took the stand in his own behalf. He was on the stand for seven days.

Marin County District Attorney Jerry Herman announced that he wouldn't file any charges against Carpenter for Kane's and Schwartz's murders due to inadequate evidence.

In 1994, potential juror misconduct in the second trial was brought to light in that the jury forewoman had known about Carpenter's convictions in Los Angeles for the Santa Cruz murders and had concealed this fact during voir dire for the Marin County trial. Carpenter was not retried as he had already been sentenced to death for other murders. On 6 March 1995 the California Supreme Court refused to give Carpenter a new trial. Justice Armand Arabian said that it was virtually impossible to keep secrets in cases such as this and that he believed that the juror's knowledge had not unduly biased the jury.

In 1997, the California Supreme Court upheld Carpenter's death sentence for the Scaggs and Hansen murders and on 29 November 199 they upheld Carpenter's death penalty from his second trial, with six of the seven justices agreeing that he had a fair trial for the five Marin County murders and had, in fact, been sentenced properly.

In December 2009, San Francisco police reexamined evidence from the 21 October 1979 murder of Mary Frances Bennett. Bennett was 23 years old at the time she was killed. She had been jogging near the Palace of the Legion of Honor in Land's End Park in San Francisco when she was ambushed and stabbed to death. Police reported that she had been stabbed at least 25 times in her chest, neck, and back. Her "butchered" corpse was found under a thin layer of dirt and leaves. In February 2010 San Francisco police confirmed that DNA collected from that murder was sent to the Department of Justice and was subsequently matched to Carpenter.

He remains a suspect in the murders of Edna Kane and Barbara Schwartz.

Aftermath

Some have speculated that Carpenter wasn't technically a serial killer but a serial rapist who killed his victims to eliminate witnesses so as not to return to prison.

Carpenter's case provided the background for Joyce Maynard's 2013 novel, *After Her*.

A series of geocaching caches have been placed throughout Mount Tamalpais in commemoration of Carpenter's victims.

TOY BOX KILLER

53

David Parker Ray was a suspected American serial killer and known torturer and serial rapist of women; suspected because no bodies were ever found. However, he was accused by his accomplices of murdering a number of women and law enforcement officials estimate that he is responsible for as many as 60 deaths in and near Truth or Consequences, New Mexico. Ray purchased and refitted a trailer into what he called his "toy box" which was replete with a number of sex toys and torture items for his victims. He also played a very disturbing audiotape for all of his victims explaining what they will be enduring at his hand. Ray was finally arrested after one of his victims managed to escape after three days of torture. Ray stood trial for kidnapping and sexual torture and was sentenced to 224 years in prison; however, he suffered a fatal heart attack while incarcerated at Lea County Correctional Facility in Hobbs, New Mexico, on 28 May 2002.

Early Life

David Parker Ray was born on 6 November 1939, in Belen, New Mexico. He was named David after his uncle David who was accidentally shot in the heart at the age of 13 by his 15-year-old brother Alden just one year earlier. Ray's grandmother believed him to be a reincarnation of her dead son.

Ray's father, Cecil, was an alcoholic and was very abusive to both Ray and his sister Peggy—who was one year his junior—as well as their mother, Nettie. When Ray was ten years old his father left his mother and moved to Albuquerque. They were divorced soon thereafter. When Nettie decided to stay with her own parents, Ray and Peggy were shipped off to their paternal grandparents, Ethan and Dolly Ray. In the six years Ray and Peggy lived with their grandparents they saw their father twice and their mother only a handful of times. Consequently, there were no maternal bonds between Nettie and her children. In fact, Ray said that he didn't get much affection or attention at all during his childhood.

Ethan was a strict disciplinarian who insisted on the utmost standards of dress and behavior and, as such, the children were required to do ranch chores both before and after school and even though the Rays were not very well off, Ethan made sure his grandchildren were clean and presentable. He was also a devout fundamentalist Christian and made sure to instill within his grandchildren his religious beliefs. Any nonadherence to his rules resulted in physical punishment.

Ray attended Mountainair High School in Mountainair, New Mexico, where he was often bullied for his awkwardness and shyness, especially around girls. Ray commented that he didn't have his first date until he was 18 years old. He was also tormented for being soft-spoken and for having to keep his shirt buttoned all the way to the top—per his grandfather's instructions—when all of the other boys had a few top buttons undone. Ray was also a poor student.

Neighbor Audie Miranda always tried to look out for Ray. He would tell the bullies to leave him alone and stated that even though Ray could defend himself, he remained docile, not liking or believing in violence which was ironic considering what Ray would become. The two became close friends and spent a lot of time together on the Ray ranch riding horses, playing cowboys and Indians, and playing desert hide-and-seek.

Ray always had a love of the outdoors.

Miranda would later say that he believed that Ray's ultra-strict upbringing took a toll on his friend. Miranda even commented that he, himself, was scared of Ethan.

Dolly was not much better. Ray said that he hated her and that she "didn't have a clue."

At the age of 12, Ray began building and setting off bombs and other explosives he fashioned in the woods behind his grandparents' house. He said he blew up a lot of tree stumps as a child.

When Ray was 13 his grandparents gave him a Cushman Pacemaker motor scooter. He discovered within himself a natural aptitude for mechanics and delighted in taking it apart and then reassembling it. The once shy and timid Ray became more confident, especially when his classmates who used to torment him needed his services to fix their scooters.

Some accounts state that Ray began to use and abuse alcohol and drugs while in high school. It was also around this time he began to fantasize about raping, torturing, and murdering women. He said that the few times his father would come visit them, he would bring true detective magazines which Ray enjoyed reading. He began having his fantasies which always involved broken bottles. His sister stumbled upon Ray's sadomasochistic drawings as well as erotic photographs of acts of bondage.

At the age of 15 Ray fashioned his own little dungeon under a large piñon pine tree with a hangman's noose and a collection of broken beer bottles he "planned to use on girls someday." He also admitted to digging a hole and engaging in intercourse with the ground when he was lonesome.

After high school, Ray worked as an auto mechanic.

He married in 1959, joking that he was practically a virgin at that time, and joined the United States Army a year later where he was sent to Korea. The Rays had a son in 1960 and Ray had to return home on emergency leave because his wife was leaving the baby alone when she went out to party. He filed for divorce and sought sole custody. His mother, Opel, and stepfather, Cecil, raised Ray's son until Ray was honorably discharged from the military.

Ray married a second time in 1962 when he was 22 years old and a mere 90 days later he went back to court and filed for divorce again because they just didn't "click".

In 1966, Ray married a third time; to a woman named Glenda Burdine. They were married 15 years and had a daughter named Glenda Jean—who would go by "Jesse"—in 1969. Jesse remembered her father as being gone quite a bit, having worked for the railroad, and of having an unusual fetish for padded leather straps and other bondage fare. She said that kids were naturally curious and while they knew about it, it was not a topic to be discussed.

In sum, Ray married four times, was divorced four times, and had two children.

Ray met Cindy Lea Hendy in 1997 when he was 57; she was 20 years his junior. Originally from Washington, Hendy and her boyfriend John Youngblood moved to Truth or Consequences, New Mexico, on the run from the law for grand theft, forgery, and drug offenses, leaving her three children behind. As she had already served time in jail, she was not keen on returning.

The Crimes

The "Toy Box"

Ray spent over $100,000 on his homemade torture chamber he called his "toy box" that he constructed inside of an old white 15-feet-by-25-feet cargo trailer on his Elephant Butte, New Mexico, property. Elephant Butte is a resort town of approximately 2,000 residents, located along an 18-mile-long, 36,000-acre reservoir.

The trailer was stocked with what he referred to as his "friends": bully whips, pulleys, leather straps, metal clamps, bars which spread the victim's legs, surgical knifes and saws which he used to torture women. Inside this trailer were also numerous sex toys, syringes, detailed diagrams that showed different methods for inflicting pain and torture, and a homemade electrical generator. Ray also mounted a mirror on the ceiling above the gynecologist table upon which he strapped his victims because he wanted them to see everything that was done to them.

He also played a recorded audiotape of himself for his victims whenever they regained consciousness. It began with:

*"Hello there, b*tch. Are you comfortable right now? I doubt it. Wrists and ankles chained. Gagged. Probably blind folded. You are disoriented and scared, too, I would imagine. Perfectly normal, under the circumstances. For a little while, at least, you need to get your sh*t together and listen to this tape. It is very relevant to your situation. I'm going to tell you, in detail, why you have been kidnapped, what's going to happen to you and how long you'll be here. I don't know the details of your capture, because this tape is being created July 23rd, 1993, as a general advisory tape for future female captives. The information I'm going to give you is based on my experience dealing with captives over a period of several years. If, at a future date, there are any major changes in our procedures, the tape will be upgraded. Now, you are obviously here against your will, totally helpless, don't know where you're at, don't know what's gonna happen to you. You're very scared or very pissed off. I'm sure that you've already tried to get your wrists and ankles loose, and know you can't. Now you're just waiting to see what's gonna happen next."*

The rest of the tape involves Ray setting forth his "rules" and "procedures" by telling his victims everything—in graphic detail—that would be done to them to include being raped and sodomized by Ray and his friends, engaging in bestiality, being shocked with electricity, and being poked and prodded with a multitude of surgical instruments and sex toys; essentially, being their sex slave to do with whatever they want. The actual recording is widely available online, quite long, and not for the faint of heart as it is extremely explicit.

In the audiotape Ray describes himself as a "dungeon master" who was affiliated with the Church of Satan and that his slaves were for members of his "congregation."

There was also a videotape showing Ray and his girlfriend Cindy Lea Hendy performing such acts of torture upon a female victim who screamed the entire time.

Psychological torture was also important to Ray. He would blindfold his victims, subject them to brainwashing, use fear tactics, and occasional small favors to keep them "off balance".

Many experts classify Ray as a sexual sadist who finds excitement and pleasure from inflicting pain upon a nonconsensual, submissive and inducing them into altered states of consciousness such as when they pass out from the pain. Such a predilection often forms during adolescence; however, experts do not know exactly what causes one to become a sexual sadist.

Ray had multiple accomplices during this time; including, allegedly, several of his girlfriends, particularly his latest girlfriend, Hendy.

During the investigation Hendy allegedly had told a friend—while she was under the influence of alcohol—that she had willingly participated in Ray's attacks because of the adrenaline rush she got from them. She allegedly confided to this person that "there were four to six people who had been killed, dismembered, and tossed into Elephant Butte Lake." While the friend did not initially believe her, after Ray and Hendy were arrested and the details of the crimes were released, he gave statements to police and the media.

Marie Parker

On 5 July 1997, 22-year-old Marie Parker and her two daughters—ages four and five—were evicted from their apartment for non-payment of rent. They were living in a pup tent on the western shore of Elephant Butte Lake at a campsite called Hot Springs Cove; just north of Ray's trailer. In fact, she had borrowed the tent from him and when her campsite became too messy for the fastidious Ray, he had something to say about it.

Parker was a methamphetamine and cocaine junkie and her main supplier was Ray's daughter Jesse. Ray abducted Parker and took her to his toy box where he raped and tortured her for three days after which he gave Yancy a rope and told him that they "were finished" with her. He then told Yancy to kill her which Yancy admitted to doing. They buried the body in a remote area and Ray threatened Yancy's life if he ever told anyone.

Later, when police took Yancy to the area where Parker's body was allegedly dumped, they could not find any evidence. Yancy stated that Ray probably moved the body.

Police found Parker's abandoned car in the parking lot of the Blue Waters Saloon.

Cynthia Vigil

Cynthia Vigil had been working as a prostitute along Central Avenue (Highway 66) at around 10:00 a.m. when her pimp introduced her to Ray and Hendy in a red recreational vehicle. Ray offered Vigil $20 for oral sex and when she entered the vehicle, Ray produced a police badge and told Vigil that she was under arrest for solicitation. Ray and Hendy handcuffed, gagged, and chained Vigil to a fixture inside of the camper. After a few minutes he pulled the vehicle over and then proceeded to cut off all of her clothing, put a metal dog collar around her neck, place her in shackles, and then slipped a leather mask over her head with no eye openings and a zipper for the mouth. She was also told if she resisted she would be shocked.

When they reached Ray's house, after driving for an hour, Vigil said that she was chained to a bed and was made to listen to Ray's infamous five-minute audiotape before being forced to have sex with both Ray and Hendy. Next, Vigil said that Ray put gravy "up" her and had his German shepherd lick it off. Vigil then had her knees attached to a bar, forcing her legs open and was then "measured" with dildoes that had markings on them before having her breasts and genitals shocked with a portable generator. The entire time Hendy had a gun pointed at her.

The next morning, Vigil was taken at gunpoint to the bathroom to relieve herself and then taken back to the bed, fresh and clean white sheets atop it, where her mouth and eyes were duct taped and she was hog-tied with an elaborate collection of interconnected leather straps. A rope was then attached to a pulley from the ceiling and Vigil's entire body was lifted three feet into the air.

The duct tape was ripped from her eyes and she saw her horrified face staring back at her from a video monitor. She said that Ray tied her legs open and proceeded to whip her with a leather belt, whips, and a cat-o' nine tails. Vigil said that the beating excited Ray who then violated her with a "horrendous looking dildo" and took pictures of her suspended body with the toys inside of her.

Later that day he attached an elaborate system of clamps and pulleys to her breasts and genitalia and proceeded to shock her. Her convulsions caused the pulleys to exert force on the clamps. After taking the excruciating pain for as long as she could, she lost consciousness.

For the next two days Vigil was subjected to sexual torture until she was able to escape.

On 22 March 1999, Cynthia Vigil escaped after being abducted by Ray and enduring a three-day torture ordeal. She was able to escape one morning after Ray had left for work and Hendy had left the keys on a nearby table when the latter went into another room to talk on the phone. Vigil—chained to the wall in the den—managed to use her legs and feet to pull the table toward her and get the keys; however, Hendy noticed her efforts and a fight ensued. Vigil was able to free herself while Hendy beat her and even after being hit in the head with a lamp, Vigil managed to stab Hendy in the back of the neck with an icepick she found on the floor. When Hendy fell to the ground, Vigil escaped the house naked save for an iron slave collar and padlocked chains, and began to run down Bass Road in Elephant Butte. Since she had just been taken three days ago, Vigil had not been taken out to the toy box yet.

Vigil was spotted by a couple of passing motorists who did not know what to make of the woman and didn't stop. Vigil finally surprised a woman at home in her trailer watching television who called the police for her. Vigil was then taken to the Sierra Vista County Hospital emergency room where the chains were cut off and her battered body was cared for.

When police went to Ray's home, they found bloodied sheets in one bedroom with a broken lamp and broken window, thus corroborating Vigil's claims. A pulley device with hooks and chains was mounted on the ceiling and there was a long, coffin-like box along the side of the bed. Large sex toys were on the dresser.

Arrest and Investigation

After Vigil's escape, Ray and Hendy were arrested off Springfield Road in his red Toyota camper. They claimed that they had kidnapped Vigil in an effort to break her of her heroin addiction. Ray and Hendy were taken to nearby

Truth or Consequences—formerly Hot Springs—New Mexico and housed in the Cooper Police Training Center.

Both Ray and Hendy were charged with 12 counts consisting of aggravated kidnapping, conspiracy, and aggravated battery and held on $1 million bail.

Soon after Ray was arrested, New Mexico State Police took the case over from the Truth or Consequences Police Department and Agent Wesley LaCuesta—a five-year veteran of the Criminal Assault and Violent Crimes Division—was called on to assist in the investigation. He left his Las Cruces office and headed north to Truth or Consequences.

LaCuesta interviewed Vigil at the hospital. He observed many small cuts on her extremities, injuries to her breasts, welts on her back, and evidence of her being handcuffed.

By early April 1999, over 100 New Mexico State Police and FBI agents were all over Ray's property looking for human remains.

Eleven days after his arrest, Patty Rust committed suicide after assisting law enforcement personnel with detailed drawings of the toy box over the course of four days. Prosecutor Jim Yontz wondered why the FBI would send a woman into a torture chamber where many women had likely been frightened to death by Ray and the torture he inflicted upon them. He then went to visit the toy box. Inside he found a ghastly collection of sex toys, medical devices, whips, clamps, chains, pulleys, rods, saws, and other items for bondage and sadomasochism; in addition to detailed drawings of how Ray liked to torture his victims, medical books on the female anatomy, and, perhaps most damning, a videotape dating back to 1993 showing a woman being tortured.

There was also a television monitor in the right corner of the toy box so Ray's victims could see what he was doing to them if they looked at the monitor while they were secured to the table. He also had a video camera focused upon the table recording everything he was doing. Photographs of the torture he had inflicted upon prior victims decorated the walls, as well as a bunch of dolls which were "strung up in various states of bondage and torture." In addition to the medical texts, Ray had a copy of Brett Easton Ellis' *American Psycho*; a novel detailing violent assaults inflicted by a man when he needed to release steam from his high-stress life that was also made into a film starring Christian Bale. The novel contains very disturbing descriptions of torture. It was presumed that Ray compared himself to the "protagonist" in the novel as he saw himself as in control and his victims as "expendable pawns in his game", even going so far as to call his victims "packages."

With respect to the videotape depicting the torture of one of Ray's victims, the police were able to find the woman on the tape: Kelly Garrett, who had been married mere days before being abducted by Ray and Hendy. Garrett had been held hostage, raped, and tortured for three days before being drugged and left on the side of the road not far from her in-laws' house. Believing Garrett had been out on a drug binge, she was asked to leave and subsequently moved back to Colorado. Investigators found her in Colorado and she stated that she had amnesia for a long time, only recently—as in the past year—remembering what Ray and Hendy had done to her.

The publicity surrounding the case prompted another victim to come forward with her story. Angelica Montano recounted her ordeal at Ray's hands just one month ago.

Angelica Montano

Montano said that she was a casual acquaintance of both Ray and Hendy and had gone to their house on 17 February 1999, looking to borrow cake mix. She said that Ray left the room and then returned with a knife and told her that she was being kidnapped. When Montano looked over at Hendy, she saw the woman holding a gun, pointed at her. She knew they were serious.

Montano said that the couple grabbed, bound, and stripped her before strapping her to a bed and placing a metal collar on her. She said they then attached electrodes to her breasts and shocked her multiple times in addition to "abus[ing] her with various sexual implements." She then said that Ray forced her to give him oral sex.

After having been chained naked to the bed for three days and being subjected to sexual abuse, it was time for Montano to visit the toy box. Ray removed her handcuffs and led her to the bathroom with a long metal leash attached to the dog collar. He bathed her "like a dog, with a chain and everything" Montano would later say. When she was clean, Hendy applied makeup to her face and then draped a robe over her captive's shoulders before Ray and Hendy led her out into the trailer.

In the smaller trailer—the toy box—Montano was strapped to a gynecologist table where she was subjected to additional electric shocks to her genitalia as well as other instances of sexual assault. She said that she repeatedly begged Ray and Hendy to release her and on the fourth day they relented. She was drugged and taken miles away from Ray's property and dumped on a local highway in the desert where a police officer found her.

Even though Montano did, in fact, report the incident to the police, there had been no follow up. When she saw that Ray and Hendy had been arrested, Montano contacted the police again.

Accomplices

In addition to Hendy, investigators discovered two other accomplices: Ray's daughter Glenda Jean "Jesse" Ray; and Dennis Roy Yancy. Yancy and Hendy had dated in the past.

Yancy admitted to strangling Marie Parker—a former girlfriend—after Ray kidnapped and tortured her. Ray videotaped the murder. Yancy also confessed to seeing photographs of one of Ray's ex-wives in various bondage positions as well as watching Ray torture a woman inside the toy box but that he thought it was consensual. Yancy was subsequently convicted of second-degree murder and conspiracy to commit first-degree murder. He received two 15-year sentences. Jesse was also tried and convicted of kidnapping for sexual torture. She was sentenced to seven years and served three, the rest of the time she was on parole.

Hendy was charged with 25 felonies and was looking at 197 years in prison. To save herself, she agreed to plead no contest and testify against Ray and Yancy in exchange for five felony counts and a 36-year sentence. In the Seventh District Court of New Mexico Hendy pled guilty to two counts of first-degree kidnapping for Vigil and Montano, two counts of sexual penetration (rape) in the second degree for the two women, and one count of conspiracy to commit second-degree kidnapping.

Over 100 FBI agents were sent to search Ray's property but they were unable to identify any human remains. Several bones were located but they proved to be of animal origin. Collecting evidence from Ray's home and toy box proved daunting due to the sheer number of items he had amassed for his tortuous pleasure. In one interview, New Mexico Public Safety Director Darren White told reporters that the evidence inside the toy box was "very disturbing stuff" and "literally made my stomach turn."

It was later discovered that Ray would drug his victims with sodium pentothal and phenobarbital to induce amnesia to prevent them from being able to report what had happened to them when they were released. In Kelly Garrett's case, she was unsure about her own recollections of the torture and accompanying nightmares; that is, until the FBI contacted her and, soon thereafter, she was able to remember—in vivid detail—what Ray did to her so she could testify against him in court.

In his recording, Ray described his whole philosophy about drugging his victims and why getting an accurate body count of those victims he killed is impossible. Ray said:

*"If I killed every b*tch that we kidnapped, there'd be bodies strung all over the country. And besides, I don't like killin' a girl, unless it is absolutely necessary. So I've devised a safe, alternate method of disposal. I had plenty of b*tches to practice on over the years, so I've pretty well got it down pat. And I enjoy doin' it. I get off on mind games. After we get completely through with you, you're gonna be drugged up real heavy, with a combination of Sodium Pentothal and Phenobarbital. They are both hypnotic drugs that will make you extremely susceptible to hypnosis, autohypnosis and hypnotic suggestion. You're gonna be kept drugged a couple of days, while I play with your mind. By the time I get through brainwashing you, you're not gonna remember a fu*kin' thing about this little adventure. You won't remember this place, us, or what has happened to you. There won't be any DNA evidence, because you'll be bathed, and both holes between your legs will be thoroughly flushed out. You'll be dressed, sedated, and turned loose on some country road, bruised, heh, sore all over, but nothing that won't heal up in a week or two. The thought of being brainwashed may not be appealing to you, but we been doin' it a long time and it works. And it's the lesser of two evils. I'm sure that you would prefer that, in lieu of being strangled or having your throat cut."*

One can only imagine the pure horror coursing through his victims' minds as they lay, chained atop his torture table, hearing—in very graphic detail—about what they will be enduring.

Trials and Convictions

The press jumped all over the case and soon discovered that everyone who seemingly knew Ray said that he seemed like a "regular" guy. He did not have any criminal record, nor were there any reports about potentially suspicious activities on his property which he leased from the park service. However, reports from the police indicated that he was considerably worse and darker than he initially seemed.

State District Judge Neil Mertz decided that Ray would undergo three separate trials: for Cynthia Vigil, for Angelica Montano, and for Kelly Garrett. The Vigil trial was set to start on 28 March 2000, in Tierra Amarilla. Judge Mertz suppressed Ray's early interviews with the New Mexico State Police and FBI and also banned the media from the voir dire. Just after jury selection, Ray allegedly suffered a heart attack and was taken to a hospital in Las Cruces. The judge postponed the trial for another week and then there were additional delays and several FBI expert witnesses were excluded.

Then, unexpectedly, Judge Mertz decided to start Garrett's trial for her 1996 kidnapping and torture even though it was the weakest case, evidence-wise. Nevertheless, Judge Mertz scheduled it for the end of May. Of course, Ray was pleased with the delays, not to mention Judge Mertz's exclusion of Ray's printed sheet of procedures for handling his slaves as well as all devices found in the trailer for Garrett's trial since nobody could prove they were there in 1996. This left the prosecution with the videotape and the victim's testimony.

When Vigil's trial was actually conducted, it ended in a mistrial because some jurors were not convinced that the women were completely held against their will and there was a subsequent retrial that resulted in convictions for all 12 counts with which Ray was charged.

Montano's trial was delayed indefinitely because, unfortunately, she was rushed to an Albuquerque hospital on 7 May 2001 with pneumonia where she died an hour later from heart failure. She was only 28 years old. As she was one of only three living, known witnesses who were going to testify against Ray, Montano's death dealt a huge blow to the prosecution. However, prosecutor Jim Yontz was prepared to try Ray for Montano's kidnapping and torture by utilizing videotaped statements she had made at a preliminary hearing on 15 and 16 April 1999.

When prosecutors started "closing in" on his daughter Jesse who assisted with some of Ray's earlier kidnappings, Ray decided to take a plea bargain. He received a sentence of 224 years in prison.

Ray suffered a fatal heart attack while incarcerated at Lea County Correctional Facility in Hobbs, New Mexico, on 28 May 2002.

Aftermath

Yancy was paroled in 2010 after serving 11 years of his sentence; however, his release was delayed because of difficulties stemming from his parole plan which had to be established before release. Three months after he was released in 2011, he was charged with violating his parole and subsequently returned to prison and required to serve his entire sentence until 2021.

Ray is suspected of murdering his one-time business partner, Billy Bowers. The two men bought, restored, and sold cars. On 22 September 1988, Bowers disappeared and his family immediately offered a $5,000 reward for any information leading to his safe return. On 28 September 1989, a fisherman found a male body floating in McCrea Canyon which is along the eastern shore of Elephant Butte Lake. The body was wrapped in a blue tarp and secured to two heavy boat anchors. It had a single bullet hole to the head and $49.47 in a pocket but no identification. There were no missing persons reports for a five-foot-ten-inch male in his late-30's or early-40's so the John Doe remained unidentified for over a decade until Cindy Hendy told police that Ray had murdered Bowers. Hendy admitted that Ray confessed the murder to her and told her that since then he had learned to open the victims' stomachs so they would "stay down" when submerged in water and not float to the surface as was the case with Bowers.

When the body was exhumed and dental records compared, the John Doe was, in fact, Bowers. His son Michael was able to retrieve the body of his long-lost father for a proper burial and some closure.

In November 2002, state police officially opened the toy box to the public in the hopes that renewed media attention might help identify additional victims. Inside were signs that said "Satan's Den" and "Bondage Room." The obstetrical table was still there with all of its clamps, leg stretchers, electric wires, chains, and straps. A steel cabinet held numerous surgical instruments and the coffin-shaped box used to terrorize and contain victims was nearby. Ray's meticulous records detailing what he did to his victims was also available. To ensure that none of his victims escaped, Ray had devised an elaborate alarm system and had written instructions to ensure that all straps were secure prior to leaving the toy box.

However, with Ray dead, the investigation went cold, especially since no bodies were ever found, no possible victims were identified, and no suspicious deaths which might have been loosely linked to Ray were solved. Despite the lack of any dead bodies, he is oft-labeled in numerous sources of literature as a serial killer.

According to Jim Fielder in his 2003 book *Slow Death*, both Vigil and Garrett went on to form relationships and start families of their own.

As recently as 2012, additional evidence has been uncovered which indicated there may be additional victims.

THE ICE KILLER AND OTHER STORIES

RAY DUNCAN

Robert Hansen was dubbed the "Butcher Baker" by the media after he kidnapped, raped and killed at least seventeen women with possibly more victims that have yet to be identified. The murders took place in and around his hometown of Anchorage, Alaska as Hansen would hunt down his victims in the woods with a variety of weapons. It would take over twelve years before authorities would finally capture and convict Hansen in 1983. His case would remain out of the limelight until a movie called "Frozen Ground" would be released, detailing his exploits with John Cusack starring as Hansen.

EARLY YEARS

Hansen was born to Danish immigrants in Estherville, Iowa in 1939. Both of his parents were strict and Robert would be crippled by shyness for his entire life. He had a stutter and a bad case of acne which left pockmarks on both of his cheeks. His father, Christian, was a baker and Robert would eventually follow him into the same occupation. But his father was not a positive influence on him, routinely belittling his son. Robert had no escape, he was bullied both at home and at school.

At school, he was the proverbial social outcast. He would walk down the halls with his eyes downcast and very few people even noticed him. He only had a small handful of male friends who kept him at arm's length and virtually no female friends.

He had no success whatsoever with the opposite sex, being alternately ignored and ridiculed. This rejection would evolve into a seething hatred of all attractive women as his sexual fantasies about them turned into violent ones.

With no outlet, he took up hunting and found solace in the woods, shooting at animals.

At the age of eighteen, Robert would join the United States Army Reserve and would serve for one year before being discharged. The army service would give him a bit of self-confidence as Robert now attempted to talk to women and ask for dates. But women were taken aback by his awkward nature, his stutter and his thousand-mile stare behind black-rimmed glasses.

With his military experience, he would find employment at a police academy in Pocahontas, Iowa as an assistant drill instructor. Once there, he began badgering a secretary for a date until she filed a complaint against him. He would eventually meet his first wife in Pocahontas, marrying her in the summer of 1960.

The marriage would not last. Only a few months later, Robert would be arrested for burning down a school bus garage.

The bullying and torment Hansen experienced during his high school years would prove to be too much. He had to somehow, someway get back at his tormentors. So even three years after he graduated he decided to go back to his old school and burn down the garage that housed the school bus.

He would be sentenced to three years in jail during which his wife would file for divorce. He would serve a little over twenty months before being released.

The arson episode would prove to be another step on the ladder to Hansen's eventual homicidal psychosis. He was showing all of the earmarks of a serial killer; arson and cruelty to animals. He had felt powerless his whole life but would act out in fantasies where he would have power...whether it was by starting a fire or shooting a deer. Eventually, this need for power would lead him to a deep-seated desire to have power over the women who rejected him throughout his life.

ESCALATING BEHAVIOR

Robert would test the waters of criminal behavior starting with petty thefts. He would be arrested several times for theft, looking to be growing into a small time criminal until 1963 when he married his second wife.

Four years into their marriage, the couple would have two children and move to Anchorage, Alaska.

Robert would start work in a local bakery. Under his father's tutelage, he was a capable baker and hiring him was a no-brainer. But his co-workers found him to be a social misfit. He would brag to them about the strangest things, like his kleptomania and ability to steal things without getting caught.

JUST ANOTHER FACE IN THE CROWD

Hansen went out of his way to give off the appearance of a respectable citizen.

His neighbors liked him and he would set several hunting records in the area, decorating his home with the heads of big game and fish. He would open his own bakery in a downtown mini-mall, becoming friends with the regular customers and even servicing the policemen who came in for their morning donut.

No one, not his wife, children or his neighbors knew of the monster that lurked inside him.

But he couldn't keep the monster hidden long. In fact, the respectable front was just camouflage.

In 1967, Hansen would assault a young receptionist at gunpoint. He would plead no contest to the assault charge but serve very little time. A few months later, he followed a pretty eighteen-year-old girl home and again tried to sexually assault her.

He would serve very little time in jail, being sent instead to a psychiatric facility where he described his bizarre and dark sexual fantasies. He would tell his psychiatrist that he suffered from memory lapses and remembered little of what took place during his assaults.

The courts were lenient on Hansen to a fault.

In 1971, Hansen would kidnap and rape a seventeen-year-old waitress outside a coffee shop.

He would let her go but not without a threat.

"I will hunt you down," he hissed in her ear. "Hunt you down and kill you. I'm a respectable man. I own a business. You're just a kid. No one will believe you."

The teenage girl, scared out of her wits, believed him.

With no punishment or capture in sight, Hansen would become even bolder as he plotted out his mouth violent fantasies.

FIRST BLOOD

In what would seem to be a recurring theme for Hansen's victims, there was very little media coverage or follow-up investigations.

In 1973, a seventeen-year-old schoolgirl named Megan Emerick walked out of a dorm laundry room in Seward, Alaska and disappeared without a trace.

She is presumed to have been another of Hansen's victims though he would later deny it.

Unfortunately, Megan's disappearance would garner little in the way of press or law enforcement investigation. There were a few fliers and short articles in the local newspaper but little else offered.

Megan was a quiet girl who grew up in the peaceful town of Delta Junction. She liked to go out on the Yukon River to hunt and fish. A typical teenager, she liked rock music and horses but she left home at an early age to go to the Seward Skill Center, a place in Alaska where she would learn a vocation.

But on July 7th, she would disappear.

Years later, the vanishing teenage girls would be part of a growing trend in the Eklutna and Knik River areas.

LOST IN THE FOG

As construction of an eight-hundred-mile oil pipeline began in Alaska, a different population began filing into Anchorage. The oil money brought in prostitutes, pimps, and drug dealers who sought to service the oil workers who now had money to burn. The community began a transient one and sudden disappearances became nothing out of the ordinary. Anchorage became a frontier town, a city full of strangers where people disappeared without a trace.

Robert would initially target any woman who caught his eye. But he began to learn that strippers and prostitutes were less likely to have people come looking for them. He would soon develop his own modus operandi, a system that he would adhere to with religious fervor.

He would target solitary women under the guise that he was a photographer, offering compensation if they posed for him. Hansen would then arrange a meeting place in a coffee shop and wait outside, making sure that the woman arrived alone. Once assured that there would be no witness, he would arrive at the coffee shop and convince the woman to come leave with him for the photo shoot. They would get into the car and he would already have one-half of the handcuff attached to the passenger side drive handle. Once he got into the driver side, he would lean over and in one motion handcuff their wrist and take out the gun from his glove compartment.

Sometimes he would drive the women home or to an isolated motel room where he would rape them. Other times he would fly to a desolate area along the Knik River.

A STRANGE CODE

Robert didn't kill all of his victims. Sometimes he would rape them and release the ones who he thought really found him attractive. His reasoning was, they played out to his fantasy and didn't deserve to die.

Others, the ones who resisted and fought, he would pretend to set free. Then he would hunt them down through the woods and shoot them with his rifle.

By the summer of 1980, bodies of dead prostitutes began to be found in and around the Anchorage area. But finding dead bodies in the Alaska wilderness was not an out of the ordinary type thing. Hikers would often get lost in the wilderness and not know how to make their way back, succumbing to the elements.

The first would be a young woman believed to be in her late teens or early twenties. Workers in a building found a shallow grave on Eklutna Lake Road. The body was badly decomposed and half-eaten by bears. Police were able to make a facial reconstruction from the skull and published their approximation of the young woman's appearance to the local news outlets. The victim was never identified, however, and to this day is still known as "Eklutna Annie."

When her body was recovered, she was estimated to be in her late teens or early twenties. She was between 4'11" and 5'3" inches tall with long, reddish-brown hair. Hansen would admit that she was the first victim that he killed but that he didn't know her name.

Hansen said that she or her family lived in Kodiak. Investigators believed that she may have come from Washington or California.

What is certain is that she was a topless dancer or a prostitute that Hansen picked up, offering to pay for her services. He told her that he lived in Muldoon but when Hansen drove past the town the woman panicked. She tried to escape out of his truck but Hansen pulled a gun on her.

"Now look," Hansen said. "If you do exactly what I tell you and don't give me any problem whatsoever, there's going to be none, you won't get hurt in any way, shape or form."

"Eklutna Annie" could only nod in agreement out of fear. They continued to drive, her heart racing with fear, her mind racing with strategies on how she could escape.

But then Hansen's truck got lodged in the wet Alaska mud. Hansen allowed the young woman to step out of the vehicle to help put the truck back on solid ground.

Then she ran.

Hansen stated that he caught her by the hair as she took a knife out from her purse.

Overpowering the young girl, Hansen wrenched the knife away and stabbed her in the back.

Her body would be found on July 21st, 1980 buried near a power line.

MORE BODIES...

Joanne Messina was another body found near Eklutna Lake Road, buried in a gravel pit. Her body was badly decomposed and there was little evidence remaining. She worked as a topless dancer as did other Hansen victims such as Sherry Morrow and Paula Goulding.

Sherry Morrow was a striking beauty, with feathered blonde hair and heart-shaped lips. She was an aspiring model who turned to topless dancing to make ends meet. Like he would do so many times, Hansen would meet her under the guise of a photo shoot.

Sherry would be among the first that Hansen would play the "hunting game" with. After raping and torturing her, he flew her to the woods where he sent her blindfolded and handcuffed, telling her to run.

His sadistic fantasies now coming to life, Hansen would hunt her down. He would follow her through the woods as she cried and begged for her life.

He shot her in the back, rolled her over and ripped off a necklace from her neck.

A 'good luck' arrowhead locket that her boyfriend had given her.

It was the next step in his mind, to begin taking mementos and trophies of his victims. He would set them aside in a box then when he felt the need to relive the moment he could take the souvenir out, fingering it through his hands and relive the fantasies in his mind.

UPPING THE ANTE...

The adrenaline high that Hansen got when he first began killing started to subside. So he began the 'hunting game' in order to feed the monster inside. He had gone from petty theft to attempted sexual assault before graduating to rape and murder.

Now it was turning the rape and murder into a sport.

Sherry's body would be found on the banks of the Knik River. Sherry had been reported missing for over a year and her body was found in a shallow grave on the banks of the river. Two off-duty police officers were in the wilderness hunting moose when they came upon her decomposed remains. She had been shot in the back three times with what investigators believed to have been a hunting rifle. Her body was fully clothed but there were no bullet holes in her clothing. Investigators believe that she had been naked when Hansen shot her after which he put her clothes back on.

Police were able to identify Sherry's body from dental records. She had been reported missing over a year ago by her boyfriend. The clothes they had found on her skeletal remains were the same as the clothes described by her boyfriend.

The case would go nowhere, however. The police told the boyfriend that the killer had over a year to cover his tracks. Finding him would be next to impossible.

Paula Goulding would meet the same fate as Sherry Morrow. Only seventeen-years-old and looking for work, the unemployed secretary started work as an exotic dancer to pay her rent. She would be targeted by Hansen and fall victim to him in the same way Sherry did. He would capture her, send her into the wilderness blindfolded where he would chase her down then after she couldn't run anymore, shoot her down like an animal.

Paula's body had been found in the exact same fashion, shot in the back but then redressed after death.

Sue Luna's body would be found two years later, the young Asian woman was forced to strip herself naked while Hansen made her run like a dog through the woods. The game was intoxicating to him as he shot her in the back after a lengthy chase.

Delynn Frey, Teresa Watson, Angela Feddern, Tamara Pederson, Lisa Futrell, and Andrea Altiery would all become victims of Hansen. He would collect "trophies" from each of them, taking a custom-made fish necklace from Andrea Altiery that would later be a critical piece of evidence when he would be captured.

But that capture when not come until June 13th, 1983 when Hansen encountered seventeen-year-old prostitute Cindy Paulson.

A STREET SMART STREETWALKER

Hansen was trolling for his next victim when he spotted Cindy selling her wares on an empty street. He had enticed Cindy to come into his car for $200 in exchange for oral sex. Cindy didn't feel threatened by the man, she got into his car without a second thought.

Hansen struck fast. He reached over and handcuffed her to the door then held a wood handled revolver to her head.

"Not a s-s-s-sound," the man stuttered as he put the car into drive. He drove her to his home in Muldoon. The alert Cindy began taking notes in her mind. The home was in a relatively well-to-do area. Once she entered, she found the home to be well kept and with nice furniture and full of hunting trophies. Hansen took her down to his den where there was a chain hanging from the ceiling. He tied her to the chain and stripped off her clothes. He would hold her captive for hours, alternating between raping and physically torturing her.

Hansen would grow tired and chained her by the neck to a post in the basement. Hansen then laid on the couch and went to sleep.

Upon awakening, Hansen untied Cindy and threw her in his car.

"If you t-t-t-try to get anyone's attention," Hansen hissed at his captive. "I will k-k-k-kill both you and them."

Hansen then bragged that he already had a rock solid alibi. He had convinced a friend to lie for him.

Hansen took his captive to the Merrill Field airport.

"We're flying out to my cabin," he snarled.

Cindy laid down on the back seat of the car, her hands cuffed in front of her body but her legs free. The car parked and she watched as Hansen began packing gear into his Piper Super Cub (a small two-seat airplane). Seeing her opportunity, Cindy scooted out of the back seat, opened the driver's side door and sprinted toward the nearest street.

Hansen turned around in time to see Cindy running but luckily for the young woman she made it to the busy street.

Robert Yount slammed on his brakes of his trucks on the rainy road. He opened up the passenger side door and picked up the young woman, immediately taken aback by her disheveled appearance. He drove her to the Mush Inn where Cindy ran inside, telling the clerk to call her boyfriend.

Yount would drive on to work where he called the police himself and told her about the half-naked, handcuffed woman he had dropped off at the Mush Inn.

Anchorage police officers arrived at the Inn but Cindy had disappeared. The clerk told them that she had taken a cab to the Big Timber Motel where her boyfriend stayed.

Police would go to the hotel and find her in room 110 of the motel. She was still handcuffed and alone. She told the police about Hansen, describing him as a wiry, scruffy man. He was tall at six feet but she thought he was non-threatening because he spoke with a stutter. She told of her hours of torture and rape, being hung up by her wrists and taken to the airport. The whole story sounded like something out of a horror movie but the detectives believed Cindy. She was street smart and scared out of her wits. The police drove her out to the hospital but then Cindy insisted on stopping by the airport.

Cindy was then able to positively identify the same plane that she saw Hansen toss weapons inside of. They also talked to a security guard who obtained the license plate of Hansen's vehicle. With a description and now an address in hand, detectives set out to Hansen's home.

Their suspect would arrive shortly after they staked out his home. Everything about him was exactly as Cindy described. He was wiry, nervous and spoke with a stutter.

As non-threatening as could be.

The inside of his home was also like Cindy as described. A moose head on the wall, trophies and news clippings of his hunting exploits.

A hidden panel in his wall would reveal a large cache of weapons.

All of this was legal, however. There was no evidence that Cindy had been raped. The only evidence was that she had been inside his home.

"I was at my friend's house," Hansen explained. "I was repairing a seat for my airplane then I went to the home of another friend. I left his house then went to the airport and installed the seat."

Hansen would deny Cindy's allegations during his interrogation. He deflected, stating that Cindy was telling them lies because he would not pay her extortion demands.

Hansen had an arrest record but his shy and quiet nature put some doubt in the mind of the cops. Police corroborated his alibi with his friend, John Henning, and the case went cold.

Cindy identified Hansen in a police lineup and insisted that he was the man who raped her. Things went south in the investigation, however, when Cindy refused to take a lie detector test. She had an inherent distrust of police and if they wouldn't take her at her word, she was willing to put the whole thing behind her.

She knew that Hansen was taking her on a one way trip to her death and she escaped. She also knew that the police didn't take prostitutes seriously.

So she walked.

She drifted in and out of the area and couldn't be reached when the police wanted to follow up. The case would be suspended.

But Detective Glenn Flothe of the Alaska State Troopers had already made the determination that the several bodies found around the area was the work of one man.

A serial killer.

And there was something about Robert Hansen that made alarm bells go off. He had a task force go out to the red light districts of Anchorage and warn the women that a serial killer was on the loose.

Then he got the FBI involved.

BRING IN THE BIG GUNS...

Flothe would team up with FBI special agent Roy Hazelwood in developing a psychological profile of the kind of man they were looking for.

Hazelwood believed that the killer was a man who was an experienced hunter but with low self-esteem. He would have a history of problems with women and would keep "souvenirs" of his kills such as a piece of jewelry or article of clothing. Hazelwood also believed that the killer would be socially awkward with a speech impediment.

Flothe used the profile and quickly narrowed down his investigation to Hansen. They would go to Hansen's home and bring him in for investigation. His team would then get a warrant to search Hansen's house, cars, and plane. They would discover jewelry belonging to the missing women as well as a cache of weapons hidden under the insulation in Hansen's attic. They would find the rifle they believed was used to kill two of the topless dancers as well as the revolver with the wooden handle he used to kidnap Cindy Paulson.

The mother lode, however, was an aviation map with little "x" marks all over it, indicating where Hansen had murdered his victims.

The search warrant was being executed at the same time that Hansen was placed into the interrogation room.

Investigators had decorated the room with pictures of his victims, maps of where they found the woman's bodies and crime scene photos.

They wanted to get inside his head, to let him know that they were on to him.

The man who psychologically tortured so many women was now having the script flipped on him.

INTERROGATION AND REVELATION

Another break in the case would come when the neighbor of Hansen noticed the police outside his home. She inquired as to what was going on and was told that Hansen was under investigation for murder. She quickly recanted her husband's story, stating that he had lied to cover up for Hansen and he did not know the extent of his crimes.

Investigators demanded an explanation of why Hansen had possession of the necklaces of the dead women. Hansen would deflect and deny until the interrogators finally cornered him. He would then get defensive, blaming the women and justifying his actions until he finally cracked.

"I started in 1971," Hansen said. "They were usually young. Like sixteen and nineteen. I didn't move to the prostitutes and strippers until later. I would get mad at them sometimes, sure. They would raise their prices on me."

Hansen would be arrested and charged with assault, kidnapping, multiple weapons possession as well as theft and insurance fraud (Hansen had filed a fake claim stating that someone had stolen his trophies. He used the proceeds to buy his private plane.)

Striking a plea bargain, Hansen would participate in telling the police about the markings on his aviation map in order to locate the bodies of his victims. He did this on the condition that they left his family alone and that it would not be publicized. An agreement was reached and Hansen would plead guilty to the murders of Morrow, Messina, Goulding and "Eklutna Annie".

"I began killing in the early 1970s," Hansen said. "Sometimes I would let the girl go. But only if she could convince me that she would not go to the cops."

Hansen would lead police to over seventeen grave sites. He would refuse to give up three marks on his map (two of these are suspected to belong to the spots where he killed Mary Thill and Megan Emrick, both of whom Hansen has denied killing.)

Hansen would be sentenced to 461 years plus life in prison without the possibility of parole. He would later be sent to the Anchorage Correctional Complex for health reasons and would die at the age of 75 on August 21st, 2014.

The identity of "Eklutna Annie" remains unknown.

STRANGLER JOHN

JOHN DENIS

John Reginald Christie was a prolific serial killer active in England during the 1940s and 1950s. He murdered at least six women including his wife—and some believe this number is higher, as well as a baby—before being arrested, convicted, and hanged. He lured women to his flat under the guise of assisting them with some medical procedure such as abortion and strangled and raped them; oftentimes while they were unconscious or dead, thus giving rise to allegations that he was a necrophiliac. Christie also likely framed his neighbor Timothy Evans for the death of Evans' wife and infant daughter for which Evans was convicted and hanged.

EARLY LIFE

John Reginald Halliday Christie was born in Halifax, Yorkshire, England on 8 April 1899. His father was a strict disciplinarian who was often abusive and mother and sisters were domineering. Yet, he was his mother's favorite so while Christie's father despised his frailty his mother emasculated him with over protection. His four older sisters also reinforced his mother's protective nature but they also dominated him. One incident when he was ten disturbed him profoundly; that of seeing one of his sister's legs up to the knee which made him physically attracted to her. This likely contributed to Christie's development into a controlling, sexually-dysfunctional hypochondriac with an intense hatred and fear of women because he simultaneously desired those who tempted him but, consequently, knew he could not satisfy them.

Christie's maternal grandfather died when he was eight and when asked if he wanted to see the body during the wake, Christie said yes. He felt pleasure and a release of the tension he always felt when the man was alive because his grandfather was rather frightening and these feelings fascinated him. He started playing in the graveyard and liked to look inside the cracks of the broken vault where children's coffins were kept.

In school, Christie did rather well and got along even though he did not cultivate any long-term meaningful friendships. At age 11 he won a scholarship to Halifax Secondary School where he proved rather adept at mathematics and algebra, and also with high-detailed work. He had an IQ of 128, was a scout, and sang in his church's choir; however, he grew increasingly unpopular with his classmates and was often ridiculed for his ineptitude with girls being given the names "Can't Make it Christie" and "Reggie no Dick." By puberty Christie had associated sex with dominance, violent aggression, and death which rendered him impotent unless he was in complete control. At this time he would also feign illness—becoming a hysterical hypochondriac—to get attention.

Christie left school at age 15 and became an assistant movie projectionist. When World War I began Christie enlisted as a signalman. He allegedly was rendered unconscious and temporarily blind by a mustard gas attack and lost his voice for three years; however, physicians attributed his blindness and muteness as a hysterical reaction instead of a true physical ailment. Thus, Christie's fear led to his hypochondria and he would exaggerate illnesses to avoid unpleasant situations. More simply, he was a coward.

After his stint in the army, Christie became a clerk. On 10 May 1920 Christie married 22-year-old Ethel Waddington from Sheffield. She was a plump, homely, passive, and sentimental woman who many believed was afraid of her husband even though he was mostly mute during this time. The couple looked down upon others and, subsequently, maintained a high degree of privacy but also seemed quiet and rather pleasant, devoted to each other, and to their dog and cat. His ongoing impotence with his wife led to his frequent visits to prostitutes—which began when he was 19—when she was out of town.

After they married Christie became a postman. He once stole some postal orders and was, consequently, sent to prison for three months. Following his first period of incarceration Christie regained his voice during a temper tantrum with his father only to lose it again for six more months before being able to speak again. When he was 25, Christie was placed on probation with the post office after being charged with violence and accused of frequenting prostitutes. Christie subsequently left his wife and moved to London while she remained in Sheffield with her relatives.

Four years later, Christie was sentenced to prison for nine months on theft charges. Following this prison release he went through multiple jobs and lived with a prostitute who he physically assaulted with a cricket bat to the head and returned to prison for six more months. He was suspected of assaulting other women; however, the lack of evidence resulted in no arrests. A few years later he stole a car from a priest and was arrested again. After being released from prison this time he asked Ethel to move to London with him so they could be a married couple again.

Thus, in 1933 after a ten-year separation—and lonely at age 35—Ethel rejoined her husband, unaware of the type of man he really was or how her life would take a tragic turn.

Soon thereafter, Christie was hit by a car and required hospitalization which fueled his budding hypochondria. The literature suggests that over the course of 15 years Christie visited two physicians 173 times.

The Christies moved to the ground floor flat at three-story 10 Rillington Place in the Ladbroke Grove neighborhood of Notting Hill. At the time they moved here, Christie was a 40-year-old quiet inconspicuous man with reddish-ginger hair, light blue eyes, and an enormous forehead.

With World War II on the horizon, Christie signed up as a volunteer member of the War Reserve Police and became a Special Constable for Harrow Road Police Station for the next four years. Had his prior record been investigated—which it wasn't—there is no way that Christie would have received this appointment. Regardless, these four years were among Christie's happiest and he became almost fanatical about enforcing the law—so much so that he earned the nickname, "The Himmler of Rillington Place." Christie enjoyed wearing his uniform so much that the authority he had inflated his ego to the extent that he began to follow women and take notes of his endeavors. He also bored a peephole into his kitchen to watch his neighbors and ran down every single transgressor, no matter how minor the offense.

When his wife went to Sheffield to visit her relatives Christie developed a taste for peculiar sexual activities and found women who responded to his advances. One woman Christie met worked at the police station with him. She had a husband overseas in the war and Christie often spent time at her house with her. When her husband returned unexpectedly he filed for divorce and named Christie as a co-respondent after beating him up upon finding Christie in his house.

After this Christie began bringing women to his flat.

But first...

Timothy Evans

In the spring of 1948 Timothy and Beryl Evans moved into the third-floor flat. They were newlyweds and expecting their first baby. Timothy was 24 and Beryl was only 19; he drove a van for a living and was functionally illiterate. Known for his excessive drinking and often violent temper—likely due to his small stature of five-foot-five and 140 pounds—as well as his IQ of 70, propensity for lying, and proneness to self-aggrandizement, the Evans frequently quarreled. When the baby arrived—they named her Geraldine—Timothy's substandard income and Beryl's poor housekeeping and mothering skills caused them to fight even more, sometimes resulting in mutual physical violence. Beryl allegedly told Mrs. Christie that Tim had tried to strangle her and that she was pregnant again with an unwanted child. Beryl tried unsuccessfully to get rid of the baby.

It was around this time—the end of October 1948—that workers came to fix some floors and walls of 10 Rillington Place, as well as the community wash house.

In early November Beryl and Geraldine disappeared. There were conflicting accounts of their disappearance and subsequent murders; however, what is known is that that Christie offered to help Beryl with her pregnancy "problem" around noon one day. He is reported to have used rubber tubing to gas her for the procedure but she allegedly panicked so Christie began to hit her, and then strangle her, and then tried to have intercourse with her. When Evans came home that evening, Christie told him that the abortion hadn't worked and that if Evans went to the police it would only get them both in trouble and that police would not react well to reports that Evans and his wife fought often.

Christie proposed that he would dispose of Beryl's body and he hid her into the second-floor flat that belonged to Mr. Kitchener who was in the hospital at the time. Evans allegedly fed Geraldine and told Christie that he wanted to take his daughter to his mother's house but was dissuaded by Christie who told him that it would arouse too much suspicion. Christie told Evans that he knew a young couple who would take Geraldine and that Evans should tell people that Beryl and Geraldine were out of town on holiday.

Some speculate that Christie strangled the baby and put her with her mother in the second-floor flat and then blocked out what he had done.

Christie then told Evans to sell his furniture and leave town which Evans did.

Once the workmen were finished in the wash house Christie moved the bodies and hid them there. The following day he visited his doctor complaining of back pain. Despite Christie being a hypochondriac he had never had back problems. The doctor concluded that it was an injury sustained by unaccustomed exertion such as lifting a heavy weight.

Evans' mother Mrs. Probert did not buy her son's account that his wife and daughter were on holiday and discovered that her son staying with her sister, awaiting his wife. Mrs. Probert knew Evans was lying, that Beryl and Geraldine were missing, and that the furniture had been sold from their flat. After being confronted Evans stated that he disposed of his wife and put her body down the drain. He said that did not kill her and did not want to mention Christie because of the additional problems that would have caused. Evans said that he had met a man who gave him some medication to produce a spontaneous abortion but told Beryl not to use it. He said that when he returned from work he found her dead, took care of his daughter, and then pondered what to do next. Evans stated that he put his wife's body down the drain outside of the front door, stayed home from work, went in to give notice, and made arrangements for someone to take of Geraldine.

Police determined that Evans could not have disposed of Beryl the way he claimed to have done and he was arrested. During his interrogation and subsequent investigation Evans claimed that that he simply helped Christie put Beryl's body in the second-floor flat and that he had inquired of Christie about his daughter but was told that it was too soon to see her. Police searched the building and garden and in Evans' apartment near a pile of papers there were clippings from the newspaper about "a sensational torso murder, known as the Stanley Setty case" which was odd because Evans did not read, as well as a stolen briefcase.

During Evans' interrogation the Christies were also interviewed, she being coached by her husband.

Police went back to 10 Rillington Place and searched again. This time they found the decaying corpse of Beryl Evans, wrapped in a green tablecloth and tied with cord in the wash house, hidden behind some wood propped up against the sink. Underneath some wood behind the door was Geraldine's dead body with a man's tie still around her neck.

Dr. Donald Teare, the Home Office pathologist, performed the autopsy which showed that both had been dead about three weeks. Beryl had bruises on her lip and right eye consistent with being hit and that she had been strangled with some type of a cord. There was no evidence that she had ingested anything to try to abort her three-month fetus but her vagina had bruising. The pathologist did not take a swab to check for semen.

Additional interrogations yielded different stories by Evans. He first admitted that he did, in fact, kill them both and that he was relieved to confess. He said he killed his wife because she was running up debts and then killed his daughter a few days later after he quit his job. On the days Evans said he hid the bodies, the carpenters were still working on the wash house so this could not be true. Further, his confession contained words that were beyond Evans' intellectual capacity and that if he had sold all of his furniture like he claimed then the baby's pram and highchair would not have been in Christie's flat—an indication that Evans expected to see his daughter again. The next confession was even longer and contradicted the first one. After Evans' mother came to see him following his arraignment he insisted that "Christie done it."

Evan's trial began on 11 January 1950 at the Old Bailey for the murder of his daughter although evidence of his wife's murder was included in the testimony. Prosecutor Christmas Humphreys wanted to avoid any testimony such that Beryl may have provoked Evans which could possibly warrant a reduced charge of manslaughter with a lesser sentence which is why he only pursued Geraldine's murder; because it was without motive and clearly cold-blooded. Christie was Humphreys' chief witness in the proceedings.

Evans' defense was in the hands of Malcolm Morris from Freeborough, Slack, and Company; however, there was little investigation done to assist Evans, likely to save on time and money. They also failed to question the carpenters and friend Joan Vincent, and neglected to look into Christie's criminal record; all of which may have provided the jury with reasonable doubt.

During the trial witnesses such as the carpenters and Mrs. Christie changed their testimony from their original statements to "fit" Evans' confessions with respect to dates and times. The furniture dealer wasn't contacted either which would have demonstrated that Evans was only following Christie's direction and that Christie had, in fact, lied. Compounding Evans' troubles was that Christie's composed persona on the stand impressed jurors due to he was articulate, reflective and presented himself as the victim. His demeanor was diametrically opposite Evans' "apparent dazed and guilt-ridden presentation." When Morris brought up Christie's criminal past the court was impressed with the fact that he had been on the straight-and-narrow for the past 17 years. Little did the court know what Christie had really been doing during that time.

It took the jury only 40 minutes to reach a guilty verdict Evans was sentenced to death and was hanged on 9 March 1950. He would later be granted a posthumous pardon after Christie's trial when the truth was revealed even though some still believe that Evans did murder his family.

The Crimes

Mrs. Christie wanted to move since the only other tenants in the flat were Jamaicans against whom she was highly prejudiced. Further, after Evans' trial Christie went into a deep depression and lost a lot of weight, and also lost his post office job due to courtroom testimony about his past crimes. Ever the hypochondriac, Christie checked himself into a psychiatric hospital for three weeks and continued to visit his doctor for stress-related symptoms; 33 times in eight months.

He found work as a clerk with the British Road Service and things seemed to improve; however, Christie soon gave notice, citing that he had found a better job which was not true. His wife was not pleased with him being unemployed and around the house all the time. On 11 December Mrs. Christie watched television with a friend, on the 12th she took laundry to Maxwell Laundries, and then was never seen again. Nobody said she appeared to be distraught or that she said that she was going to take a trip.

Christie told her friends that she went to Sheffield and that he would follow shortly as he had a new job there. He told family members that his wife wasn't feeling well enough to write them.

At this same time Christie began to sprinkle his house and garden with disinfectant due to the increasingly putrid odor.

In January, Christie sold his furniture along with his wife's wedding band and watch. For more money he forged his wife's signature on a bank account she had and emptied it.

Shortly thereafter Christie met a Mrs. Reilly who was looking for a place to rent and he showed both her and her husband his flat. They paid him three months' rent in advance and kept his cat. Christie borrowed a suitcase, had his dog put down, and left. The Reillys ultimately left when the impending investigation commenced and they were told that Christie did not have the authority to sublet his flat.

Investigation

One of the upstairs tenants at 10 Rillington Place—Beresford Brown—noticed a hollow space behind a kitchen wall in Christie's old flat after the landlord gave him permission to use the kitchen since the flat was empty. Brown was looking for a place to mount a shelf for his radio and pulled away some of the wallpaper to try to open the door which he couldn't. When he shined a light through a crack he was horrified at what he found and called the police.

Chief Superintendent Peter Beveridge was on scene, as was Chief Inspector Percy Law of Scotland Yard, other officers, and the coroner. When the door was opened in the kitchen alcove they found a woman's corpse sitting in some rubble. Her back was to them and she was leaning forward. Behind her was something large wrapped in a blanket that was knotted to the victim's bra. Said bra was pulled up around her neck along with her black sweater and white jacket. Other than that she was nude save for a garter belt and stockings. She was taken from the cupboard and photographed and examined in the front room. She had been strangled with a ligature and her wrists were tied in front of her with a handkerchief tied into a reef knot.

Authorities focused on a second large object behind the woman and discovered it was another corpse. It had been propped on its head up against the wall. The blanket had been fastened with a sock tied in a reef knot around the ankles and the head was wrapped in a pillowcase that was also fastened by a stocking in a reef knot.

They noticed a third object. It was another body, also upside down, with her head beneath the second body. This one's ankles were tied with an electrical cord fashioned into a reef knot while a cloth covering her head was similarly knotted.

Investigators also took note of some loose floorboards in the rubble and found the wrapped body of Mrs. Christie amidst the rubble.

The first victim was a 20-something brunette who had been deceased for approximately one month. She had died from carbon monoxide poisoning and strangulation with a smooth type of cord. She had been sexually assaulted either at the time of her death or shortly thereafter. Scratches on her back indicated that she had been dragged across the floor. She was later identified as Hectorina McLennan, a 26-year-old prostitute.

The second victim was also a brunette and around 25 years of age. She, too, exhibited symptoms of carbon monoxide poisoning; particularly her pinkish skin color. She was also strangled and had had sexual intercourse around the time of her death. There was also evidence that she had been drinking heavily the day she died. She had poorly manicured hands and feet and was clad in a cotton cardigan and vest while another vest was fashioned into a diaper between her legs. It was estimated that she had died eight to 12 weeks earlier. She was later identified as 26-year-old Kathleen Maloney, also a prostitute.

The third victim was a mid-20s blonde, also poorly manicured, clad in a dress, petticoat, bra, cardigan, two vests, and another cloth fashioned into a diaper. She had also been poisoned with carbon monoxide and strangled. She, too, had been drinking before her death which was also eight to 12 weeks earlier and this victim was six months pregnant. She, again, a prostitute, was identified at Rita Nelson, 25.

The final victim—found under the floorboards—was a woman in her 50s, plump, and missing several teeth. She was rolled up in a flannel blanket with a pillowcase over her head. She was also wrapped in a flowered dress and silk nightgown and wore stockings. She had been dead approximately 12-15 weeks. She had been strangled by ligature but unlike the others there was no evidence of gas poisoning or sexual intercourse. She was identified as Ethel Christie.

Additional evidence found in the flat included potassium cyanide, a man's tie fashioned into a reef knot in the kitchen cupboard, a man's suit under floorboards of the common hallway, and a tobacco tin that contained four clumps of pubic hair; none of which belonged to any of the victims. From where Christie obtained the hair has never been resolved.

Police also found a human femur in the garden supporting a wooden trellis. Additional bones were uncovered in flowerbeds and beneath an orange blossom bush along with blackened skull bones with teeth, pieces of a dress, a newspaper fragment dated 19 July 1943, hair and teeth, and one skull. The coroner determined that there were two female corpses although only one skull had been found.

Forensic evidence enabled these last two victims to be identified as 21-year-old Ruth Margarete Fuerst who had arrived in England from Austria in 1939 and had disappeared 24 August 1943. She was around five feet seven inches with a tooth crown identified as being from Germany or Austria. When she disappeared she had been living in Notting Hill. The second victim was presumed to be Muriel Amelia Eady, 32, who had worked with Christie in a factory. The hair in Christie's garden matched hair from her former home. The black wool dress she was wearing when she disappeared matched remains in Christie's garden.

After Christie's failed affair with the woman whose husband was overseas, he didn't have any problems finding women who would, in fact, appreciate his attention. One day in a bar he met Fuerst. She worked in a factory and was also rumored to have been a prostitute. When Mrs. Christie was away she began to visit Christie at his home. One day in bed, Christie received a telegram telling him that his wife was on her way home with her brother. Christie alleged that Ruth had undressed voluntarily and asked him to have sex with her and then they could run away together. He stated that he refused and strangled her while they were having intercourse. He wrapped her in her coat and put her under the floorboards in the parlor until after his brother-in-law left and Mrs. Christie went to work. Christie then put Fuerst in the wash house and began to dig in the garden. That night he buried her in the garden. He found some of her clothing peeking up from the shallow grave and burned it.

It is hypothesized that Christie's lifelong hatred for women and repeated humiliations caused him to act the way he did. By strangling his victims he was able to exert some semblance of power and this was erotic for him as he was only able to achieve potency with women who were helpless: that being unconscious or dead. He admitted that after he killed Fuerst he experienced "a strange, peaceful thrill."

Christie met his second victim, Eady, in the company canteen as they both worked in the same factory. In October 1944 when his wife went to Sheffield to visit relatives Christie lured Eady into his house by telling her that he had a first-aid background from when he was with the War Reserve and could help her with the catarrh (mucous buildup in her nose and throat) from which she suffered. To avoid a struggle he was prepared with a contraption that resembled an inhaler with friar's balsam in a jar to mask the gas smell and a hose connected to the gas supply. Eady sat in a chair with a scarf over her head and as she inhaled, the carbon monoxide took effect; thus enabling Christie to strangle her with a stocking while simultaneously having intercourse as she was dying. He recounted experiencing the same peaceful thrill he had with Fuerst. Christie hid her body in the wash house and dug a shallow grave near the first. Later he found a broken femur bone while gardening and used it to prop up the trellis—something the police had not seen when they were investigating Timothy Evans for his wife's and daughter's murders.

Necrophilia is defined as having sexual relations with the unconscious or dead and keeping them close. There are three identified types. One is the violent variant wherein the perpetrator has an overwhelming urge to be near a corpse so they kill in order to satiate this urge. Often the individual visits the corpse where it is dumped and in some cases there is repeated sexual contact. Another type is the fantasy necrophiliac who makes death a central aspect of his or her erotic imagery. These types may ask a partner to play dead or take pictures of him or her looking dead so they can masturbate later. Christie is a textbook fantasy necrophiliac because, as mentioned, he was unable to perform absent the violence when he murdered his victims. He also had a violent necrophilia orientation in that he did, in fact, keep his victims nearby: in the alcove in his flat, under the floorboards, in his garden, and in the building's communal wash house.

Arrest

After Christie left his old flat he placed his borrowed suitcase in a locker and wandered around London. On 20 March 1953 he checked into a room at the King's Cross Rowton House with his real name and address. Despite booking seven nights he only stayed four. When a photograph of him emerged wearing his raincoat he purchased an overcoat from another man and gave him his raincoat instead. While he claimed at trial that he was in a daze, aimlessly wandering around London, his actions demonstrate that his contriving a disguise of sorts proved otherwise. He also claimed that despite news stories about corpses found at his house, he did not connect them with himself.

Out of money, Christie took to sleeping on benches and in movie theaters and was spotted by a police officer on 31 March near the Putney Embankment of the Thames River. After giving the officer a fake name and address, Christie was asked to remove his hat and was, subsequently, recognized and promptly arrested. On his being were his identification card, his Union card, an ambulance badge, a ration book, and an old newspaper clipping about the Timothy Evans trial with details about the murders.

Christie willingly gave his statement about four of his murders. He hinted that he couldn't remember something, essentially making the police "show their hand" by admitting that they did, in fact, find the two bodies in the garden. With respect to his wife Christie claimed that she had awakened him one night and she was choking; her face was blue. He tried to restore her breathing but she was suffering so badly that he got a stocking and strangled her to put her out of her misery. He then said that the bottle containing the phenobarbitone tablets he had been prescribed for insomnia was almost empty and he realized that his wife took the pills to kill herself. After leaving his dead wife in their bed for a couple of days he put her under the floorboards, admitting that he thought this was the best way to put her to rest and keep her close to him.

He managed to make the other three women's murders not his fault either. Since they were prostitutes he claimed that they were the aggressors, demanded money, and forced themselves into his flat. He claimed Nelson picked up a frying pan to hit him and they struggled and she fell into a chair "that happened to have a rope hanging from it." When Christie came to from his alleged blackout she was dead. He said he left her there overnight and in the morning—after he had a cup of tea—he wrapped her up, diapered her, and shoved her into the alcove cupboard.

With respect to Maloney, Christie said that he met her in a café and she went home with him and threatened violence and only remembers her being on the floor and that he put her into the cupboard. In reality, he gassed her, strangled her, had intercourse with her, and then diapered and wrapped her body.

Christie stated that McLennan and her boyfriend needed a place to stay so he invited them to live with him. He asked them to leave after "several uncomfortable days" and she had come back one night, struggled with Christie after he asked her leave; however, some of her clothing tore and got wrapped around her neck. He said he sat her in a chair but she appeared to be dead so he put her in the cupboard.

The numerous psychiatrists who evaluated Christie while he was in Brixton prison described him as "nauseating" and "sniveling" and he would whisper answers to questions he did not like; not unlike his demeanor during Evans' trial. He also allegedly dissociated when describing his actions, referring to himself in the third person; however, he boasted about his actions to other inmates saying that his "goal" was 12.

Trial, Conviction, and Execution

When faced with the myriad evidence against him, Christie quickly admitted to killing his first two victims but hesitated to take responsibility for Beryl Evans who he later admitted that he did, in fact, kill but not baby Geraldine. He said Beryl's was a mercy killing like his wife as a result of a botched suicide attempt on her part. Christie alleged that Beryl offered him sex to help her but he could not perform. None of the evidence corroborates Christie's account.

Christie's trial for murdering his wife commenced on 22 June 1953 at the Old Bailey. He pled not guilty by reason of insanity. His own attorney, Derek Curtis-Bennett, even called Christie a maniac and madman which was supported by Dr. Jack Abbott Hobson, a defense psychiatrist. The prosecutor's psychiatrists said that while Christie had a hysterical personality it was neurosis not a defect of reason and, therefore, Christie was not insane.

After a mere four-day trial and an 80-minute jury deliberation Christie was found guilty and sentenced to death. He did not appeal and was hanged at Pentonville Prison on 15 July 1953.

GIRL STRANGLER :

THE TRUE STORY OF SERIAL KILLER

DANA SUE GRAY

ERIN PIERCE

Dana Sue Gray was born on December 6th, 1957 in Pasadena, California. Her mother, Beverly Arnett, was a former beauty queen who worked as a professional model. Her father, Russell Armbrust, worked as a hairdresser and was married three times prior to marrying Beverly. The couple had several miscarriages before Dana was born.

Her mother was born for the camera and loved attention. She liked being pampered, getting her make-up done and wearing flashy outfits. Beverly modeled for Bullock's, did print ads for Hamilton watches and was once a Rose Princess at the Tournament of Roses Parade.

LIKE MOTHER LIKE DAUGHTER

Russell divorced Beverly, however, when he witnessed his wife attack an older woman that had angered her. Beverly had also maxed out his credit cards, putting him financial peril. Dana was only two years old at the time of the divorce and rarely saw her father.

"Some kind of estrangement had taken place," forensic psychologist Lora Dixon said. "After her parents divorced she had turned down invitations in her teen years to visit her father on all of the holidays and birthday get-togethers."

"There is also something to think about here in terms of Beverly's own temper. Dana clearly witnessed violence and bullying from her mother at an early age. She inherited those characteristics from her mother with tragic results."

Dana had discipline problems early on as she sought attention from her narcissistic mother. Her mother would discipline her but Dana would retaliate by stealing money to buy candy. Her mother had two other children from a previous marriage. Dana would go into the rooms of her step brothers and urinate in their beds.

Her mother would continue to try and discipline her to no avail as Dana would lash back with violence. This facet of her personality was never placed under her control.

"Mommy and daughter didn't get along," Dixon said. "But obviously that isn't unusual nor does mean she was destined to become a serial killer. There was some deep seated issues festering here though. This is evident when Dana gave her mother a snake for Christmas. 'A snake for a snake' the card must have read."

Nonetheless, it did not appear on the surface that Dana had to endure the brutal childhood that gave birth to so many other serial killers. Cedric Ward, one of her step brothers, did admit that Dana did not have the best of childhoods. "It was not happy growing up," he recalled.

SCHOOL AND SEX

Dana did not get along with other students and achieved low grades in all of her classes. She was a chronic truancy case and often forged notes to get out of class. Dara was sexually active at a very early age as she would lose her virginity at the age of twelve. She would ultimately go from one relationship to the next, using sex to lure men into her web of narcissism.

"Dana has a problem," said Richard Singer, a boyfriend of her mother. "She does not want to be told no. She has her own thing, and nobody could tell her any different. You could not tell Dana what to do."

"Her mother would pretty much try to control her, but Dana would go off on you. You could not tell her what to do. Dana is very hyperactive and opinionated."

During her adolescent years, she loved horror movies and read Grimm's Fairy Tales numerous times. As a teenager, she and a neighbor built a catapult. They would tie tiny parachutes on the cat's backs and then hurl them into the air, with the parachute carrying them down into neighborhood swimming pools.

A MOTHER'S DEATH

Beverly contracted breast cancer when Dana was fourteen. Dana decided to become a nurse after witnessing the way the nurses at the hospital treated her mother. Her mother died and Dana was forced back to live with her father.

"The temptation here is to say that Dana was inspired to become a nurse by witnessing the compassion the nurses shown her mother during her illness," Dixon said. "But I would posit a different psychological scenario. Dana saw that the nurses had power over her mother. That for once, her mother was weak and had to defer to other people for the first time in her life. Dana wanted power. Control. What better way to get that then to become a nurse?"

Dana went into a depression after her mother died and would reveal her sentimentality in letters she would write to her then boyfriend, Don Lane, in jail.

"Tomorrow, Good Friday, 4-1-94, is also April Fool's and also my real mom's 76th B-day. It's been 22 years since her death, and I still celebrate her B-day for her. I celebrate it for her 'cause she died when I was 14 and we never got to get past the 'grow years' to become friends like my dad and I are. She was wild-but made my younger years a total adventure: camping, clamming @ Pismo, best Halloween parties and the best Xmases a poor family could have. She could make a fun time out of just anything."

"Again, you see in her letters a sense of victimhood," Dixon said. "She makes no mention of her mother ignoring her birthdays. And she describes her family as 'poor.' They lived in relatively affluent area, becoming strapped for cash primarily because of Beverly's spending."

GROWING UP

Dana's father Russell had remarried, living with his new wife Yvonne who had a daughter named Cathy. Dana would move in with the couple, sharing a room with Cathy. The reunion between her and her father would be a short-lived one, however, as Yvonne would find marijuana in Dana's room.

Russell's wife then kicked Dana out of the home.

On her own at the age of fifteen, Dana would move-in with her sky-diving instructor, Rob Beaudry. The union would produce two pregnancies but Rob talked Dana in to getting abortions both times. These were decisions that she would later come to resent.

At five-foot-two and weighing a stocky 135 lbs, Dana would nonetheless inherit her mother's penchant for fancy clothes and desire to be pampered with manicures and pedicures. Despite her taste in high-end living, associates would describe her appearance and demeanor as "hard."

She would graduate from Newport High School in 1976 and enter nursing school at Saddleback College in Mission Viejo, California. Dana paid her way through nursing school while working as waitress. She also taught herself screen printing techniques and sold screen printed items for extra cash.

"Dana inherited her mother's psychology when it came to money and relationships," Dixon said. "She operated from a 'lack mindset', in that she always saw herself as poor. She was industrious but felt sorry for herself that she had to work so hard, paying her way through school and working for a living. The shopping sprees were a relief to her perceived burden."

ESTRANGED FROM FAMILY

Dana became estranged from her half-brothers, her older siblings from Beverly's previous marriage. The reasons were always financial as she become embroiled in a dispute over the proceedings from their aunt's estate.

She had run-ins with her half-brother Rick in particular.

Dana reacted with anger after he told her to sell belongings to pay her mounting bills. Rick wrote back telling her that she had no consideration for others.

"Nuts," is how her sister-in-law described her. "Not even normally greedy. Crazy. Gray is missing a conscience. I do not think it is there. When you talk to her, she has no concept of other human beings."

"The half-brothers clearly knew she was trouble," Dixon said. "They did the right thing in distancing themselves.

NURSING CAREER.

Immediately upon graduating from Saddleback, Dana landed a nursing job at Corona Community Hospital. She used that as a springboard to a high paying position as an operating room nurse at Inland Valley Regional Medical Center (some reports have her identified as a labor and delivery nurse). She was described by one nursing supervisor as "very caring."

During this time, she had found another boyfriend, a windsurfer whom she would accompany on trips to Hawaii where they would pursue various outdoor activities. This relationship would be an on-again, off-again type deal until Dana would marry Tom Gray. The couple would tie the knot at a winery in the affluent Temecula area.

Tom was an active sportsman and had a crush on Dana since high school.

"She was a hard core athlete," Tom recalled. "A sky diver, wind surfer, mountain bike enthusiast and snorkeler, and she was skilled in each sport."

Dana took pride in her physical strength and would often roll up her sleeve to reveal her bicep muscle. 'She how strong I am?' she would ask.

Living in the gated community of the affluent Canyon Lake suited Dana as it would have been something that would have pleased her mother. Her and Tom started numerous businesses where they used the name "Graymatter."

Tom could not stop Dana's spending habits, however. The couple took out a loan for $47,000 and another for $20,000 within the first nine months of their marriage.

"She was replicating the marriage of her mother and father," Dixon said. "She liked the empowerment that came from having a lot of money. Having money, or rather the act of spending money is what fed her ego. Only in Dana's case she took it way beyond her mother. She was willing to kill for that feeling."

The marriage quickly soured when Dana's spending habits sent the couple into overwhelming consumer debt. Her alcoholism also worsened, particularly after she suffered a miscarriage. Dana indulged in three or four glasses of wine while cooking dinner and then having more with the dinner itself. Her days off from the hospital were adventures in bourbon whiskey, 7-Up and Tequila shooters. Later, she would admit to using marijuana and cocaine.

When Gray unexpectedly received a $7500 inheritance, Dana took the money and blew it on a trip to Europe, leaving her husband behind at home. When she returned , she began an affair with Don Lane, a musician in her husband's band. When Lane agreed to support her, she moved out of the Canyon Lake house and spent $11,000 in five months.

In March of 1992, however, Dana began seeing a psychiatrist. He prescribed Paxil for her, probably to stave off depression among other things.

Lane had a five year old son at the time and would later tell authorities of Dana's "mood changes" and her propensity to break out into "hysterical tears" with little provocation.

She filed for divorce from Tom but this would not be finalized until much later. In September of 1993, Tom and Dana were forced to file for bankruptcy to prevent foreclosure on their Canyon Lake residence.

Despite the value of the home increasing, the amount they owed on the house was more than its worth. They owed $177,500 on a house valued at $125,000 because of double mortgages.

She suffered a miscarriage, exacerbating more depression as well as alcohol and drug abuse.

FIRED FROM THE HOSPITAL

The trouble continued for Dana as two months later she would be fired from the hospital for stealing Demerol and other opiate pain killers.

"What Dana was trying to do was medicate herself," Dixon said. "The new marriage, the exotic vacations, the fancy house and cars. It was never enough to quell the demons that spoke in her head. A control freak out of control. So she struggled to constantly fill the void with booze and drugs. Then this spirals into an affair with a friend of her husband. Again, this life trajectory happens to a lot of people. In Dana's case, however, she needed that extra thrill. Something more than the rush of sky-diving, cheating on her husband, and getting high. She needed the ultimate adrenaline rush. The power to take someone's life."

TIME TO KILL

In later reports, hospital authorities would reveal their own problems with Gray.

"She is sarcastic," Darlena Addison, the former nursing supervisor who fired Gray for stealing drugs. "She does get her point across if she's crossed or doesn't get her way."

"The problem was a condescending attitude, as Dana believed that she was smarter than everyone and had a need to dominate."

The hospital would later report that they did not have any "unusual" deaths during Gray's tenure.

"Of course that is what you would expect them to say," Dixon said. "If they admit to any 'unusual' deaths then it certainly opens them up to a lawsuit. The opportunity would certainly be there for Dana to steal credit cards from elderly patients and rack up bills. It appears, however, that she did not put her murderous impulses into action until after her dismissal. Dana fell in love with the struggle. The fight of her victim as long as she would emerge on he winning end. Poisoning her victims to death in the way it would have been possible for her as a nurse would not have given her that adrenaline rush."

After the loss of her job, Dana would amp up her indulgences in alcohol, drinking straight Vodka, loving the Smirnoff brand in particular.

On Valentine's Day in 1994, Dana contacted Tom's parents (after their separation he had kept his phone number and address a secret). She informed Tom's parents that she wanted to meet with him.

Tom agreed at first but later did not show up.

Tom would find out that Dana had taken out an insurance policy on him without his knowledge. The policy payout would have been enough to pay down the Canyon Lake home the couple used to share.

Later that day, Dana murdered Norma Davis.

THE FIRST VICTIM

Norma Davis was 86 years old at the time. She was the mother-in-law of the woman (Jeri Davis Armbrust) who married Dana's father in 1988. Jeri's first husband, Bill Davis, was Norma's son. Bill died in the early 1980s, and his widow married a newly divorced Russell.

But Jeri continued to care for her elderly mother-in-law, even after she remarried. Dana would also come to know Norma very well.

On February 16th, 1994, however, the body of Norma Davis would be found by a neighbor named Alice Williams. She had been dead for two days as someone had stabbed her in the neck with a wood-handled utility knife. The blade had been inserted so deep that it nearly severed Norma's head.

She also had a filet knife sticking out of her chest.

Police would discover no forced entry into the home. Norma always kept the doors locked unless she was expecting a visitor. Her neighbor, Alice, stated that she could not remember if Norma had mentioned she was expecting company.

"We didn't have a lot of information," Detective Joe Greco said. "The only piece of evidence that we had was the entry way of the condominium. There was a faint shoe print on the condominium and it was a 6 ½ size shoe."

Detectives would find the Nike shoe print and Davis' Social Security check in plain view. Additionally, on the first floor of the condo, they found a smear of blood on an armchair and a torn phone cord.

A modus operandi had been established. Dana would manually strangle her victims with a phone cord, then use an object to smash or stab.

The coroner concluded that Norma Davis was strangled first then stabbed. She was stabbed eleven times with Dana leaving the knives stuck in her body.

Police described the scene as one of the most brutal they had ever encountered.

"It was a shock because it was only my second homicide case as a detective," Greco said. "It was overwhelming. It crossed my mind that I had a serial killer on my hands."

SHE DEVIL ON A RAMPAGE

"The community was very affluent," Greco said. "They don't have a lot of homicides."

On February 28th, 1994, 66-year old June Roberts was found murdered. She had lived in the gated community of Canyon Lake along with Dana.

Dana had known Roberts and visited her that day saying that she wanted to borrow a book about either overcoming alcohol addiction or vitamins, the reports vary. Dana had her boyfriend's five year old son waiting out in front in her Cadillac.

Ignorant of Dana's true motives, Roberts allowed Dana into her home. She went to retrieve the book Dana inquired about while her would-be killer ripped out the cords to June's phone

Dana would later describe their interaction taking a turn when she became "really annoyed" that June came back with the wrong book. She also told a psychologist that she became infuriated that June allegedly said that she "didn't do enough" to save her marriage with Tom.

When asked what made Dana believe that Roberts and her other victims were looking down on her, Dana responded that she did not like their body language.

"The arching of the eyebrow," Dana said. "That is what happened. All three."

Dana then used the phone cord to strangle Roberts to death.

"I was right behind her," Dana recalled. "I choked her with the phone cord. She was holding on, trying to get the cord off. I pulled her down. She was on her back. I hit her in the head with a bottle. I lost it. I was so consumed. I don't know the time span in there-must have been very quick. She must have stopped moving, and I left. As I walked out, she had a little wallet thing. I grabbed it."

"We went out and proceeded to shop up a storm. "

In talking to psychologists,.Dana appeared unaware of the concept of remorse.

"It was very brutal," Greco said. "The victim had been strangled with her own telephone cord and actually tied to a chair. And she was struck so hard (by the wine bottle) she fractured her skull."

Her autopsy noted a "moderately deep ligature furrow" and a "6 x 3 purple contusion." The cranium contusion was caused by a heavy glass wine bottle striking her with tremendous force. The volume of blood in and near the bathroom door, the walls and pooling under the body made it impossible to gauge the age of the victim.

"This is when the profile of Dana Sue becomes highly unusual," Dixon said. "With female serial killers, you usually see poison or the use of a gun as the weapon of choice. Dana Sue, however, approached her victims with a high level of physical violence that rivaled a male serial killer. There was nothing lady-like about her approach. She was a cold blooded, hands on killer."

TIME TO SHOP

Dana did not hesitate after murdering Roberts, she had to get her shopping fix met.

She would go to Bally's Wine Country Cafe in Temecula, eat crab cake and scampi while charging the meal to Robert's credit card. She could not finish the entire meal, however, and had the waitress pack the rest.

She then got an eyebrow wax and a perm then treated her boyfriend's son to a stylish haircut.

"The fact that she had the little boy accompany her on both the murders and the shopping trips deserves mention," Dixon said. "Dana remained childless throughout life. She was regretted getting two abortions and suffered a miscarriage during her marriage with Tom. Going out and about with her boyfriend's son made her feel like a Mommy. She could be the Mommy that she never had, treating the young child to things she always wanted."

Dana signed "June Roberts" on the $164.76 charge at the salon. She then went to the mall and spent $511 on a black suede jacket, several pairs of cowboy boots, and then $161 on a pair of diamond earrings all charged to Roberts. Her addiction still not satiated, she went to a drug store, picking up dog treats, two bottles of Smirnoff and a toy police helicopter for the boy.

The day after, Dana loaded up on suntan lotion, got a massage at Murrieta Hot Springs resort and then went on another power shopping spree.

"She had absolutely no remorse," Dixon said. "There was no hiding out and laying low like some other wimpy male serial killer. Dana Sue was different. She killed and then she had to do the one thing that gratified her. She had to get to the mall. She had to get the high from buying stuff. She had to enjoy the power while it still lasted."

Ironically, none of her victims had anything stolen aside from their credit cards.

"Dana didn't take any rings from her victims," Greco said. "Or some valuables from the home that were obvious. So I don't think any of the crimes were motivated by money."

Ten days after the Roberts' murder, Dana would enter an antique store, the Main Street Trading Post in Lake Elsinore. Dana stated to the cashier, Dorinda Hawkins, that she wanted to buy a picture frame for a photo of her deceased mother.

"Dana came in asking about picture frames," Greco said. "During their interaction, Dana felt that Dorinda was being condescending to her."

"I felt sick to my stomach," Dana said. "I wanted to vomit. I wanted her to die."

Dana asked if Hawkins was working alone and then she attacked her, strangling her with the store's telephone cord.

"Dorinda is begging for her life when Dana is strangling her," Greco said. "And Dorinda told her 'you can have anything you want. Take the cash, I have eight kids, just let me live.' And Dana told her 'I'm not doing this for the money.' She said that twice. And that really gives you an insight on what Dana is thinking while she's committing these crimes."

Dorinda, however, continued to fight, resisting Dana all the way.

"Relax," Dana said, trying to coax Hawkins into dying. "Just relax."

Hawkins grabbed a broom and poked Dana with it to no avail.

Dana then shoved Hawkins to the ground and stepped on her head as a brace to better choke her.

"Her eyes were flat," Hawkins recalled. "I could tell she had killed before."

Believing her victim dead, Dana stole five dollars from Hawkins' purse and twenty dollars from the cash register.

An hour later, she began another shopping spree, still using Roberts' credit cards.

Hawkins, however, would survive the attack and provide the police the required description of Dana.

THE ATTACKS CONTINUE

Nearly a month after her first killing, on March 16th, 1994, Dana would kill the 87-year old Dora Beebe.

Moments after Beebe arrived home from a doctor's appointment, Dana pulled up in front of her house. She knocked on the door and asked Beebe for directions.

"Here we see Dana getting bolder," Dixon said. "With Norma Davis and June Roberts, she knew the victims beforehand. And the attempted murder in the antique store seemed to be a spur of the moment thing. But the Beebe murder is the first occasion where Dana has picked out a stranger. Elderly women were her preferred target, specifically those who were alone, and tragically Beebe emerged in her cross-hairs."

Living in the same neighborhood for several years, it was improbable for Dana to become lost. But she used that as an excuse when she came knocking on Beebe's door asking for directions.

Dana became angry when Beebe said "I don't have time for this." She was able to hide her anger as Beebe capitulated and allowed Dana insider her home to look at a map. Once inside the home, however, Dana assaulted the elderly woman.

'She turned her back on me," Dana said. "I choked her with the phone cord. I hit her in the head with an iron. As I remember it, it wasn't much of a fight."

Using a stainless steel Black and Decker iron that Dana found in the home, Dana bashed Beebe in the head so hard that it dented the appliance.

Less then an hour later, Dana would be at the mall with Beebe's credit cards in hand.

"She enjoyed doing things that were risky," Greco said. "She was a thrill seeker. I think that she really enjoyed what she was doing. She got a thrill out of it."

PANIC IN THE STREETS

The residents in the gated community of Canyon Lake went into panic mode. Some of the elderly citizens moved in with family until the killer was caught. A group of elderly widows organized themselves to sleep together at designated houses, not wanting to be alone.

There were some who thought the killings where the product of a cult engaging in the ritual sacrifice of the elderly.

"Rumors circulated around the entire community," Dixon said. "A terrifying time for everyone, the elderly in particular. This was a relatively well-to-do neighborhood. People were unused to killings, let alone a serial killer. Numerous people bought guns and kept it by their bedside while others banded together in the belief that there were safety in numbers."

FALSE SUSPECT

Police detectives were at a loss early on in finding a suspect. Prospects were so bleak that a supervisor in charge had seriously thought about using a psychic. Dana was not anywhere near the police's list of possible killers. Instead, the police initially suspected that her mother-in-law, Jeri Armbrust, might be the killer.

The police determined that Armbrust used to be married to Davis' son and continued to care for her former mother-in-law.

Detectives grew suspicious because it was unusual that Jeri would continue to take care of someone who was not a blood relative. Norma Davis herself was on death's door, recovering from a triple bypass surgery.

Police determined that Jeri had been in Davis' house the Sunday before the murder and that she wore a pair of Nike shoes.

Jeri stated that she did come to Davis' house but only came to drop off groceries. She heard the TV on upstairs but did not go up to say hello. She left the groceries on the counter and went home.

Police questioned why she didn't say hello but after weeks of questioning police determined that Jeri was not a suspect. She instead became an ally to the investigation.

CAPTURE

Descriptions obtained from the various merchants at the shopping center were eventually used to catch Dana. She had been buying so much stuff that the credit card company called June Roberts' family to inquire about the excessive spending.

Police detectives went to all of the stores where Roberts' credit card had been used, interviewing the cashiers. They obtained a physical description of Dana, surmising that the killer had dyed her hair recently and was accompanied by a little boy.

Detective Greco relayed this information to Jeri Armbrust.

Jeri surmised that the killer was in fact, her step-daughter Dana. She said that Dana recently dyed her hair red and had a boyfriend who had a young son.

Greco then obtained a search warrant and called for the aid of ARCNET (Allied Riverside County Narcotics Enforcement Team) to stake out Gray's home in Lake Elsinore.

Unfortunately, Dana was murdering Dora Beebe just hours before they determined her to be the killer. They followed Dana to a bank where she used Beebe's credit card and then went out for another shopping spree.

"We were able to follow the paper trail created by the use of these credit cards," Greco said. "With the merchants we were able to get a general description of the suspect."

Later that day, Greco arrested Dana while she was cooking dinner. Assisting officers took her boyfriend and his son in for questioning.

HOUSE OF STOLEN GOODS

Police did a thorough search of Dana's home after her arrest.

"They found jewelry, food, liquor, a ski mask, a purse with nearly $2,000 stuck in the washing machine, and many items of clothing," one report stated. "The police obtained a wealth of evidence: Gray's use of credit cards, clerks who had seen her directly after each murder, handwriting experts who identified her signatures on various items."

Dana was interrogated for hours.

"In the interview," Greco recalled. "Dana talked about finding a purse. And that purse belonged to a woman by the name of Dora Beebe. I knew that I had the right suspect in this case. But I didn't not know that on the same day we were serving her search warrant she was killing her last victim."

Dana stated that she never took the credit cards but after police revealed that they had evidence of her using them, Dana claimed that she found both Roberts' and Beebe's cards.

She maintained this story throughout the questioning. When asked why she kept the cards she said that she "had an overwhelming need to shop."

NO REMORSE, NO SYMPATHY

Dana displayed no sympathy for the victims. One psychologist noted that some of Dana's answers were like a robot answering in a manner they believed a normal human should.

After a hearing, Deputy District Attorney Richard Bentley wanted the death penalty. Dana pleaded insanity for all charges. But a witness came forward and stated that she saw Dana at Roberts' house on the day of her death, Dana quickly changed her plea to guilty and robbing and murdering two women as well as the attempted murder at the antique shop.

"At the end of the day," Dixon said. "Dana didn't want to die. When a witness came forward and said she saw Dana at the Roberts' house perhaps she knew that she was done for and would have been executed. Maybe she did not have enough confidence in her ability to pull off the insanity defense. So she struck a deal. She would plead guilty and avoid the death penalty."

Nonetheless, prosecutors were still unable to determine how Dana left the bloody crime scenes without a speck of blood on her or any sign of a struggle. All the clerks and waitresses spotted nothing out of the usual.

LIFE WITHOUT PAROLE

On October 16th, 1998, Dana Sue Gray was sentenced to life without parole.

"It's hard to find words to describe the atrocity in this case," Judge Patrick Magers said during Dana's sentencing. "The crimes were horrendous, callous and despicable."

Dana is currently jailed at the California Women's Prison in Chowchilla.

"She enjoyed the power," Dixon said. "She got addicted to the power she obtained while she killed people who were helpless to fight back. She liked watching them struggle. Liked having control over them before they died."

Jail has not seemed to bother Dana as she referred to her incarceration as her "county condo." She continues to pester her jailers to replicate her high-maintenance civilian lifestyle. She insists on a vegetarian diet and wants the use of a chiropractor. She has requested a mirror and has lobbied consistently for the return of her belongings.

Dana has drawn chilling clown faces, cobbling her paints together from M&M's candy coating, cherry drink mix, lipstick and and baby powder.

Her family came to visit her and brought her a pair of cheap Nike's. She refused them, wanting the high-end models.

Dana continues to thumb her nose at authorities as she sometimes sends collectibles to "murderablia" websites. She has sold her panties at $250, where she autographs them and writes in her prison identification number. She sells her hand tracing for $65 and a 'prison worn shirt', decorated with a drawing of a blue butterfly perched on a skeleton's hand.

"We can look back and say that she was simply psychotic," Dixon said. "And it is really easy to dismiss her killings as someone who was simply crazy violent and not read into it anymore than that. But in looking at the ages and gender of the victim, we can see the connection. All of her victims were old enough to be her mother. So perhaps in Dana's mind she saw her victims as substitutes for her late mother with whom had a lot of anger toward. And I mean violent, aggressive anger. So when she subdued her victims with the phone cord, she would unleash a torrent of rage, smashing them with irons, stabbing them with utility knives,bashing them over the head with wine bottles. She would attack them and have flashbacks of her battles with her Mom, doing things to the victim that she was powerless to do to her mother as a little girl."

"She was doing it all for Mommy."

THE HILLSIDE STRANGLERS

NAOMI ROBERTS

Cousins Kenneth Bianchi and Angelo Buono, Jr. are collectively known by their media epithet "The Hillside Strangler". These two men were responsible for the murders of at least nine females, ages 12 to 28, during the late 1970s in Los Angeles, California, and Bianchi killed two more in Washington. After their first three victims did not gain much attention because they were prostitutes, Bianchi and Buono decided to abduct and murder middle-class "nice" girls. Five victims were found on hillsides in the Glendale-Highland Park area during Thanksgiving weekend in 1977 and the resulting panic led to the coining of the moniker "Hillside Strangler".

Lead Los Angeles Police Department homicide investigator Detective Sergeant Bob Grogan, along with his partner Dudley Varney as well as Los Angeles Sheriff's Department's Detective Frank Salerno, believed that the murders were the work of more than one killer but figured the less the murderers knew about what police knew the better.

Bianchi later moved to Washington where he murdered two more women before being caught.

Both Bianchi and Buono were convicted of multiple counts of first-degree murder and sentenced to life. Buono dies of a heart attack on 21 September 2002 while serving his time in Calipatria State Prison in Calipatria, California. Bianchi continues to serve his sentence at Washington State Penitentiary in Walla Walla.

Early Lives

Kenneth Bianchi

Kenneth Alessio Bianchi was born on 22 May 1951 in Rochester, New York, to a 17-year-old alcoholic prostitute who gave him up for adoption two weeks after he was born. He was adopted by Nicholas Bianchi and Frances Sciolono and despite a stable upbringing, Bianchi became a pathological liar at a very early age. Further, as a result of petit mal seizures he suffered at the age of five, Bianchi often daydreamt as if he were in a trance.

Bianchi suffered from insomnia and frequently wet the bed as a child (one of the triad symptoms of serial killers). Frances took him to the doctor on multiple occasions for his urination problem and being examined by the doctor caused Bianchi much embarrassment and humiliation. He also had a bad temper and was diagnosed with passive-aggressive personality disorder which is characterized by an individual who may appear to be enthusiastic about and actively comply with others' desires and needs while simultaneously resisting them, thus resulting in increased anger and hostility. At the core of this disorder is that the sufferer resents responsibility and instead of openly expressing his or her feelings, demonstrates said resentment through actions such as procrastination, forgetfulness, and inefficiency. Despite having a rather high IQ of 116, Bianchi was a chronic underachiever in school. When Frances took him to a psychologist, it was determined that Bianchi was overly dependent upon his mother.

On 2 January 1957, Bianchi fell off of a jungle gym and landed on his face. His mother then sent him to a private Catholic elementary school where he excelled in creative writing. In July 1963, Bianchi pulled down a six-year-old girl's pants after "spontaneously decid[ing] that he liked doing so".

His adoptive father died in 1964, thus leaving an unemotional Bianchi having to attend public high school where he joined a motorcycle club and dated frequently. His adoptive mother was forced to work and she was known for keeping Bianchi home from school for extended periods of time.

While in high school, Bianchi set high standards for his many girlfriends such as complete fidelity and outwardly absolute devotion; however, these standard did not apply to him.

He graduated in 1971 from Gates-Chili High School in Rochester and, soon after, married his high school sweetheart, Brenda Beck; however, the couple divorced after only eight months. Rumor has it that Brenda left without a word.

Bianchi enrolled at Monroe Community College to study police science and psychology after deciding that he wanted to become a police officer; however, after only one term he dropped out and then was rejected for several positions both in Rochester and, later, Los Angeles. Consequently, Bianchi worked a series of menial odd jobs, eventually becoming a jewelry store security guard for which he was fired for stealing and giving his girlfriends the stolen jewelry. He would steal from other employers over the years.

He then left Rochester and moved to Los Angeles in late 1975 at the age of 26.

Angelo Buono, Jr.

Angelo Anthony Buono, Jr. was born on 5 October 1934, also in Rochester, New York, to first-generation Italian-American immigrants originally from San

Buono, Italy. His parents divorced when he was young and a five-year-old Buono moved to Glendale, California, with his mother Jenny and his sister Cecilia, where his mother supported the family by doing piecework in a shoe factory. Raised Catholic, this had no effect on Buono's development as a decent human being.

Buono displayed a very high interest in sex from a young age and when he was a teenager claimed that he had raped and sodomized number of girls. Buono idealized serial rapist Caryl Chessman, also known as "The Red Light Bandit", calling Chessman his hero but added that Chessman should have murdered his victims. He developed a deep loathing of women and desire to injure and humiliate them, including his mother who he would verbally abuse; however, he was emotionally tied to her until her death in 1978.

Buono began stealing cars and was sent to the Paso Robles School for Boys.

In 1955, Buono married his high-school sweetheart, Geraldine Vinal, who was 17 years old at the time, who he had impregnated; however, less than a week later he left her. She would later give birth to a son, Michael Lee Buono, on 10 January 1956. Buono filed for divorce and refused to pay child support or let his son call him "Dad". He was back in jail for car theft when his first son was born.

Later, he impregnated Mary Castillo who gave birth to his second son, Angelo Anthony Buono III, at the end of 1956 and then married her in 1957. The couple would have four more children: Peter in 1957, Danny in 1958, Louis in 1960, and Grace in 1962. In 1964, Buono was believed to have sexually assaulted his two-year-old daughter Grace; however, there is insufficient literature to know fully the circumstances of the allegation. Buono's second marriage to Castillo also ended in divorce that same year after she purported that he had been physically, emotionally, and sexually abusive toward her. In a last-ditch effort to reconcile with him, Castillo was "rewarded" with his handcuffing her and threatening to kill her at gunpoint. Castillo would later recount a night during the first year they were together where Buono tied her spread-eagled to the bedposts and "raped her so violently she was afraid that he was going to kill her" and "her pain seemed to him his greatest pleasure" and, thus, he had no qualms of hurting her and didn't seem to care that the children witnessed the abuse. He avoided paying child support again.

Buono married a third time in 1965 to a 25-year-old single mother named Nannette Campino and the couple had two children of their own: Tony in 1967 and Sam in 1969. Despite being treated as poorly as Mary Castillo had been, Campino feared for her life on a daily basis but stayed until he began to sexually abuse her 14-year-old daughter. Buono allegedly bragged that he raped his stepdaughter because "[s]he needs breaking in" and then turned her over to his sons for their pleasure. Campino finally took her children, filed for divorce, and fled the state in 1971.

Buono, again, was arrested for auto theft and was sentenced to one year in prison; however, due to his large family his sentence was suspended so he could work to support them.

Buono married yet again, on a whim, to a woman named Deborah Taylor; however, the couple did not live together, nor did they ever divorce.

In 1975, he became a car upholsterer and purchased his own place at 703 E. Colorado Street to live and work. Despite his abuse, cockiness, overbearing nature, and lack of good looks, Buono was considered very attractive by women, particularly younger ones who were usually naïve about sex so it was easy to convince them that his outrageous demands and proclivities were normal. Thus, he frequently forced women to engage in sex acts with him and began a relationship with a teenage girl whom he twice impregnated.

He was ugly inside and out; very coarse, vulgar, ignorant, selfish, and sadistic.

Bianchi and Buono Together

At the age of 41, Buono came into contact with his cousin Kenneth Bianchi, the latter who, in 1975, moved to California and in with his cousin. Bianchi found his older cousin with "dyed black hair, gold chains around his neck, a large gaudy turquoise ring on his finger, red silk underwear and a virtual harem of jailbait girls". Buono taught Bianchi how to use fake police badges in order to coerce free sex from prostitutes. When they needed money the two also became pimps for a short time until the two girls who worked for them—Sabra Hannan and Becky Spears—escaped after enduring relentless abuse by Buono. Bianchi, still desiring to become a police officer, applied for jobs at the Los Angeles Sheriff's and Glendale Police Departments but neither were hiring. He then procured employment with a title company and used his first paycheck on an apartment and a Cadillac, moving in with coworker

Kelli Boyd. Boyd rejected his marriage proposal as she considered Bianchi to be very jealous, immature, and a liar; however, in May 1977 she told him she was expecting their first child together. The couple moved to an apartment at 1950 Tamarind Avenue in Hollywood.

Bianchi also rented some office space and set himself up as a psychologist with a fake degree and credentials. He did not have many clients and when Boyd found out she was outraged. During the "Hillside Strangler" investigation, Bianchi told Boyd he had lung cancer and was undergoing chemotherapy and radiation to explain for his work absences; however, this was a lie. One day, detectives came to his apartment to ask questions but were "favorably impressed" and did not consider him a suspect at that time.

The Murders

In October 1977, the two men committed their first murder together. Their M.O. was to cruise around Los Angeles and use fake badges to convince women that they were undercover police officers. After persuading them into Buono's car that the men said was an unmarked police car, the two would take their victims to Buono's house where they would rape, torture, and strangle them with their "signature" weapon—a garrote (a handheld ligature such as a chain, rope, or strap)—although some of their victims were reportedly killed by lethal injection, electric shock, and gas asphyxiation. Their bodies were thus disposed of outside, frequently in hilly areas.

Yolanda Washington, 19

19-year-old tall, leggy, African-American prostitute Yolanda Washington disappeared on 17 October 1977 from Cathedral City, California. She was found the next day dumped just outside Forest Lawn Cemetery, beaten, raped, and strangled with a piece of cloth. Her corpse was cleaned and there were faint marks around her wrists, ankles, and neck. Her body was posed in a grotesque sexual position.

Judith Lynn Miller, 15

On 31 October, 15-year-old Judith Lynn Miller, a runaway, was found in a La Crescenta-Montrose neighborhood, face up on a parkway in a residential area. The homeowner covered her with a tarp so that neighborhood children wouldn't see her. After the incident, that same homeowner relocated his family to another state.

The victim was small and thin, perhaps 90 pounds, with medium length reddish-brown hair. She had bruising around her neck. She had also been raped and sodomized and her body had been posed with her legs in a diamond-like position.

Los Angeles Sheriff's Department Sergeant Frank Salerno was called to the site. He noticed insect activity upon her skin and on her eyelid was "a small piece of light-colored fluff" that he saved for forensic experts. He surmised that she had been killed elsewhere and her body had been deliberately placed where it would quickly be found.

At her autopsy, the coroner determined that she had been killed around midnight and was raped and sodomized.

There was no missing person's report matching this latest victim so after a couple of days, Salerno had the newspapers run a small story on her with a request to contact the police if anyone could identify her. Still nothing. Salerno then took her picture to Hollywood Boulevard and showed it to hundreds of runaways, addicts, homeless people, and prostitutes. The name Judy Miller kept coming up as a young destitute prostitute. One man named Markust Camden—a self-proclaimed bounty hunter—told Salerno that he saw Judy Miller leave the local fish and chips restaurant at 9:00 p.m. the night before she was found dead. In fact, he would pick Buono out of a police photo lineup, but failed to recognize Bianchi.

Eventually, Salerno was able to track down the Miller family and got a positive identification. They had nothing useful to contribute to the investigation.

Elissa "Lissa" Teresa Kastin, 21

Lissa Kastin, 21, was working as a waitress at the Healthfaire Restaurant to pay for ballet lessons as she was an avid dancer. She also worked part time for her father's real estate and construction business. She was last seen leaving work the night of 5 November. She was found the next day near the Chevy Chase Country Club in Glendale on 6 November; which was also near to where Buono lived. She had been beaten, raped, and strangled to death.

Salerno compared notes with the Glendale Police Department and noticed similarities between his latest victim and this new one. Both bodies had the same five-point ligature marks—ankles, wrists, and neck—and had been dumped within six miles of each other. This latest victim had been raped but there was no evidence of sodomy.

When Salerno looked at the dump site he was confident that at least two men were involved due to the large guardrail between the street and where the body was found and the near impossibility that one man could have gotten her body over it alone.

Dolores Cepeda, 12 and Sonja Johnson, 14

After their early murders failed to attract much publicity, Bianchi and Buono decided to find some younger victims.

12-year-old Dolores Cepeda and 14-year-old Sonja Johnson were abducted in Highland Park, California, on 13 November. They had last been seen getting off a school bus heading home from St. Ignatius School and approaching a large two-tone sedan that, reportedly, had two men inside.

Both young girls were found on 20 November in the hills between Glendale and Eagle Rock, near Dodger Stadium by a young nine-year-old boy who was treasure hunting in the trash on the hillside.

Los Angeles Police Department Homicide Detective Dudley Varney had been called to this site.

Kristina Weckler, 20

That same day, 20-year-old Kristina Weckler was found on the other side of the same hillside where Cepeda and Johnson were found.

Weckler was a quiet, loving, and serious honors student at the Pasadena Art Center of Design and lived in Glendale.

She was found nude, raped, tortured, and strangled to death as evidenced by ligature marks on her neck, as well as around her wrists and ankles. She had blood oozing from her rectum and bruises on her breasts. Weckler was the first victim to show additional overt signs of torture; having been injected with Windex glass cleaner she had oozing injection marks on her arms.

Los Angeles Police Department Homicide Detective Sergeant Bob Grogan—Varney's partner—was called to this site. He noticed that there was no indication of any disturbance of the foliage in the area or evidence that the body had been dragged there. Grogan made a mental note that she likely had been killed elsewhere and then carried and dumped in this location by one or maybe two men.

At this point, police were entertaining the idea that there was more than one killer and that they were becoming increasingly more sadistic.

Jane Evelyn King, 28

28-year-old actress Jane King disappeared in Los Angeles around 10 November 1977, and was found near the Los Feliz off ramp of the Golden State Freeway on 23 November. She had been sodomized and strangled and her body was badly decomposed. After King was found, Los Angeles Police Department officials—in addition to Glendale Police Department and Los Angeles County Sheriff's Department officers—created a task force to catch the "Hillside Strangler".

Lauren Rae Wagner, 18

18-year-old student Lauren Wagner lived with her parents in the San Fernando Valley. Her parents had gone to bed on 28 November, expecting their daughter to return home before midnight. The next morning, they found her car parked across the street with the door ajar.

Wagner was found later that day in a wooded area near Glendale's Mount Washington area. She was lying partially in the street, nude, with ligature marks on her ankles, wrists, and neck. Wagner, too, had been tortured as the palms of her hands contained several burn marks.

At the dump site was also a "shiny track of some sticky liquid, which had attracted a convoy of ants". Police considered that if the substance was saliva or semen from the killer then, perhaps, his blood type could be determined, as tests on semen found inside the earlier victims revealed nothing. It was later found that Bianchi was not a secretor, in that his blood type could not be determined by other bodily fluids. DNA testing had not come into popularity at this time.

When Wagner's father questioned the neighbors, it turned out that the woman who lived in the house where his daughter's car was parked, Beulah Stofer, saw Wagner's abduction. Stofer said that Wagner had pulled over to the curb at around 9:00 p.m. and two men had parked their car beside hers. After some type of disagreement, Wagner "ended up in the car with the two men".

When Grogan went to talk to the neighbor, she told him that she had just had a phone call from a man with a New York accent who told her to "keep her mouth shut about what she had witnessed or he would kill her". Stofer also told Grogan that the car was a large dark sedan with a white top and that one of the men dragged Wagner from her car into his while Wagner protested, "You won't get away with this!" Stofer described one man as tall and young with acne scars while the other was older and shorter, Latin-looking, and with bushy hair. She said she was positive that she would identify them again. This statement rang true when she picked both Bianchi and Buono out of a photo lineup shown to her by Grogan.

Kimberly Diane Martin, 17

Tall, blonde prostitute Kimberly Martin, 17, disappeared from Echo Park, California, and was found strangled to death on 13 December 1977 on a steep hillside on Alvarado Street. Martin had worked for the Climax "modeling agency".

Police believed they had two reasonably good leads in this case. First, Martin's last "client" called her to 1950 Tamarind, apartment 114; however, this turned out to be a vacant apartment. Secondly, the murderer called from a payphone in the lobby of the Hollywood Public Library on Ivar Street. Unfortunately, nothing came from these leads.

Cindy Lee Hudspeth, 20

On 16 February 1978, 20-year-old Bible school teacher and secretary at an Echo Park church Cindy Hudspeth was found in the trunk of her bright orange 1977 Datsun B210 that had been pushed over a cliff on Angeles Crest in Los Angeles National Forest near La Canada. She had been raped and strangled, with the strangulation marks similar to those associated with the "Hillside Strangler".

Hudspeth was also a neighbor of Weckler even though the two women did not know each other. Interestingly, Bianchi also lived in the same apartment complex; however, this lead was never pursued even though both Grogan and Salerno believed that there was a good chance that at least one of the murderers lived in the Glendale area.

After this case, the lack of additional victims resulted in the disbanding of the "Hillside Strangler" Task Force.

Jill Barcomb, 18 (originally believed to be a Hillside Strangler victim)

18-year-old prostitute Jill Barcomb was abducted in Beverly Hills and found near the famous Hollywood sign on 9 November. Whereas it was originally believed that she was a victim of the "Hillside Strangler" because she had been raped, beaten, and strangled, in 2005, her death was conclusively proven through DNA analysis to have been committed by Rodney Alcala, the "Dating Game Killer".

Also, sometime in 1977, the two men gave Catharine Lorre a ride with the intent of killing her; however, when they learned that she was the daughter of famous actor Peter Lorre who played a child murderer in Fritz Lang's 1931 masterpiece film *M*, they let her go. She had no idea who the men were until they were arrested.

The two stopped killing after their ninth victim, Hudspeth (although at this time it was presumed they had ten victims with Barcomb), likely due to the birth of Bianchi's son and, as some surmise, that he had made some acquaintances within the Los Angeles Police Department who would take him on ride-alongs around the city, ironically, looking for the killers, and Bianchi could talk about nothing else while in police presence. On the night they had tried to abduct another victim, the two men got into a heated argument when Bianchi told his cousin that he had been questioned in the "Hillside Strangler" case. After Bianchi's confession about being questioned by police, Buono, furious, threatened to kill his cousin.

Bianchi's Washington Murders

Bianchi's girlfriend, Kelli Boyd gave birth to their son, Sean, in February 1978, and in March Boyd decided to return to her parents in Bellingham, Washington, as she was tired of both Los Angeles and Bianchi's lifestyle. After three months of pleading to be reunited, Boyd relented and Bianchi moved to Washington in May. Bianchi's role as boyfriend and father was relatively successful and he even took a job as a security guard, ultimately earning the trust of his supervisors. However, this way of life did little to alleviate Bianchi's murderous urges. Within six months he was actively looking for new victims.

On 11 January 1978, Bianchi lured two Western Washington University students—roommates Karen Mandic, 22, and Diane Wilder, 27—to a house he allegedly "guarded" under the pretense of housesitting. Once there, he raped, tortured, and murdered them.

On 12 January, police were informed that two female students were missing after Mandic's boss became worried that she didn't arrive at work that day. He did remember that she had told him she had accepted a housesitting job in a wealthy Bayside neighborhood from a security guard friend of hers. When former-priest-turned-Bellingham-Police-Chief Terry Mangan went to the girls' home he found a hungry cat, as well as the address of the home where they were to housesit. The name of one security guard kept coming up, as well as a record that Bianchi had used a company truck that same night, supposedly to take into the shop for repairs. This never happened. Mangan began to consider the fact that the women had met with foul play.

Police then went to the Bayside house and found a wet footprint. They also interviewed a neighbor who told them that a security guard asked her to check on the house except for the night the women disappeared because "there was special work being done to the alarm system and he didn't want her to be taken as an intruder".

After a press conference, a woman called police to report that a car had been abandoned near her home in a heavily-wooded area. In the car were the bodies of Mandic and Wilder. Both had bruising and had been strangled to death.

Mangan had the security guard picked up. He gave them no trouble. His name was Kenneth Bianchi.

There was ample forensic evidence in this case; most notably foreign pubic hairs on the girls and fibers from the house's carpet matching fibers on the dead girls' clothing and shoes. Additionally, when police searched Bianchi's home they found several items stolen from job sites where he worked.

Remembering back to the "Hillside Strangler" cases in Los Angeles—and knowing Bianchi had lived there—Mangan called the police departments in California who had worked on the task force. He spoke to Detective Frank Salerno to whom everything finally made sense. Detectives tirelessly worked to link Bianchi to the strangler cases and were confident that he was one of the murderers.

Investigation and Arrest

Bianchi was not as careful this time, having left significant clues, most notably his car with California license plates was seen and subsequently connected to the addresses of two Hillside Strangler victims. Without mastermind Buono, Bianchi didn't have the wherewithal to cover his tracks.

Bianchi was arrested the following day, on 12 January 1979.

Buono was arrested on 22 October 1979, after Bianchi told police about his cousin's complicity in the murders.

Trial and Conviction

Prior to his 1981 trial, Bianchi decided to plead not guilty by reason of insanity and claimed to have a separate personality named "Steve Walker" who had committed the murders. After several interviews by experts specializing in multiple personality disorder and hypnosis, it was determined that he was faking. Immediately after Dr. Martin Orne mentioned to Bianchi that in genuine cases of multiple personality disorder there are typically at least three personalities, Bianchi created another alter ego named "Billy", shortly followed by two more. It was later determined that the name "Steven Walker" came from a student whose identity Bianchi had previously tried to steal to enable him to fraudulently practice psychology. Further, in Bianchi's apartment investigators found several psychology books which laid credence to Bianchi's ability to fake the disorder. He was eventually diagnosed with antisocial personality disorder with sexual sadism.

During trial, there was significant physical trace evidence against the two men; including fibers from Buono's upholstery from his home and workshop on two of the victims; an imprint of a fake police badge on his wallet; and hairs from rabbits he had raised on another victim.

Bianchi agreed to plead guilty and testify against his cousin in order to get leniency, albeit uncooperatively (evidence of his passive-aggressive personality disorder).

Judge Ronald M. George—who would later become California Supreme Court Chief Justice—said during Buono's sentencing hearing, "I would not have the slightest reluctance to impose the death penalty in this case were it within my power to do so. Ironically, although these two defendants utilized almost every form of legalized execution against their victims, the defendants have escaped any form of capital punishment." On an interesting side note, George's roommate at the time was author Darcy O'Brien who, four years after the trial, wrote a book about the case.

Both men were sentenced to life in prison.

While incarcerated, Buono married mother-of-three Christine Kizuka in 1986 while she was visiting her husband—and father of her children—who was in the cell next door to Buono at the Los Angeles County Jail, serving 18 months for assault with a deadly weapon. She worked as a supervisor at the California State Employment Development Department.

Whereas the 64-year-old Bianchi continues to serve his life sentence at the Washington State Penitentiary in Walla Walla, Buono died of a heart attack on 21 September 2002 while serving life at Calipatria State Prison in Calipatria, California. Denied for parole on 18 August 2010, Bianchi will next be eligible for parole in 2025.

Aftermath

Bianchi is also a suspect in the "Alphabet Murders"—also known as the "Double Initial Murders"—which occurred in the early 1970s in his hometown of Rochester wherein three young girls were raped, strangled to death, and dumped in the wilderness. At the time he worked as an ice cream vendor situated near two of the murder sites. On 16 November 1971, ten-year-old Carmen Colon disappeared and was found two days later in Churchville, New York, 12 miles from where she was last seen. 11-year-old Wanda Walkowicz disappeared on 2 April 1973 and was found the next day in Webster, New York, off State Route 104, seven miles from Rochester. Finally, on 26 November 1973, Michelle Maenza, 11, disappeared and was found two days later in Macedon, New York, a mere 15 miles from Rochester. They were called the "Alphabet Murders" because not only did the young victims have the same initial for their first and last name but they were also found in cities which began with the same letter.

Whereas Bianchi has repeatedly tried to get his name cleared from these murders he remains a suspect because his vehicle was seen near two of the murder sites.

Another series of murders with similar circumstances occurred in California in the late 1970s and investigators have hypothesized that they are connected to the Rochester "Alphabet Murders". In 1977, Roxene Roggasch, Paula Parsons, and Carmen Colon (like one of the original "Alphabet Murder" victims) were found raped and dead. Whereas Bianchi was tried for six murders, DNA exonerated him of the California "Alphabet Murders".

A 2008 movie entitled *The Alphabet Killer* was very loosely based upon the murders, and in 2010 a book written by Cheri Farnsworth called *Alphabet Killer: The True Story of the Double Initial Murders* was released.

In 1980, Bianchi started a relationship with a Veronica Lynn Compton, who was a defense witness during his trial. Compton, a cocaine addict who was fascinated by serial killers, was working as a scriptwriter in Hollywood.

On one of her numerous visits with Bianchi while he was incarcerated, she gave him a copy of her screenplay entitled *The Mutilated Cutter*, about a female serial killer, and asked for this input. Compton grew increasingly fixated and allegedly fell in love with Bianchi. Later, she was convicted and incarcerated for attempting to strangle a cocktail waitress who she had lured to a hotel in a ploy to have the world—and authorities—believe that the real "Hillside Strangler" was still on the loose and that the wrong man was incarcerated. To make it look like an authentic "Hillside Strangler" murder, Bianchi manipulated and used Compton as a means to get out of prison by giving her semen of his smuggled out of the facility in a rubber glove to plant on the body. Despite that DNA forensics had not been utilized at that time, semen could still be analyzed to demonstrate the killer's blood type; however, Bianchi was not a secretor. The intended victim managed to get away and Compton was tried and convicted of first-degree attempted murder and sentenced to life. Compton was paroled from prison in 2003.

In 1992, Bianchi sued Catherine Yronwode for $8.5 million for putting an image of his face on a trading card. He claimed his face was his trademark. The case was dismissed with the judge saying that if Bianchi's face was, indeed, his trademark during the murders then he would not have tried to hide it from police.

In 2007, Buono's grandson, Christopher Buono, shot his grandmother—Mary Castillo who was married to Buono at one time—and then committed suicide. Christopher was unaware of his grandfather's true identity until 2005.

Bianchi and Buono are immortalized in film. The 1989 film *The Case of the Hillside Stranglers*—based on O'Brien's book—starred Dennis Farina as Buono and Billy Zane as Bianchi. In the 2004 film *The Hillside Strangler*, Buono was portrayed by actor Nicholas Turturro and Bianchi was portrayed by C. Thomas Howell.

The 2006 movie *Rampage: The Hillside Strangler Murders* starred Tomas Arana as Buono and Clifton Collins, Jr. as Bianchi.

In 2001 the Discovery Channel aired an episode of *The New Detectives* that revisited the murders.

Bianchi and Buono have also been mentioned several times on the television show *Criminal Minds* as an example of killer teams with psychopathic predatory sexual sadist personalities who murdered their victims together.

ROADSIDE STRANGLER

JASMINE GREY

When one envisions a serial killer, they think of a cold, calculating, heartless monster. As humans, some of us have developed ways to recognize other humans that are looking to cause us harm. If we look at a mug shot of famous another serial killer, like Charles Manson or Jeffery Dahmer, one could say that these men "look" like serial killers. Maybe it's because of their wild eyes, the way that they hold themselves, or the "creepy" feeling one receives from their presence. These factors are enough to make a person stay as far away from the killer as possible, but sadly, not all predators come with a warning sign. Michael Bruce Ross, later to be known as the Roadside Strangler, was a ruthless predator that slipped under the radars of the multiple women that he attacked, raped, and murdered. Detective Malchik, Ross' arresting officer, described this serial killer as, "There was nothing threatening about him, there was no signal to any of these people that there was a dark side or something that they should be afraid of. He was able to conceal that until it became time for him to attack these innocent, young women." Ross seemed to be an average-looking man of completely average-strength and abilities, but underneath his calm and normal exterior beat the heart of a man who struggled with his sadistic, sexual compulsions. When someone spoke to Michael Ross, they would say that he put off a very friendly and articulate demeanor seemed very well educated and kind, but it was merely a costume that he had created over a lifetime. The creepy part about Michael Ross, despite how honest and upfront he is about his murders, is the mystery behind his words. Is he being genuine or is this merely an act? Is he being honest or are we being deceived? His state of mind drifts from monotone claims to not possess any remorse for his monstrosities to genuine pleas for a chemical castration to reduce his perverse sexual desires. Michael Bruce Ross' case was a strange one, to say the least, and his mental condition will forever be remembered as a very dark part in Connecticut history.

The Childhood

Michael Bruce Ross was born on July 26, 1959. Among three other children, Michael Bruce Ross was born into the life of a middle-class chicken farmer. His mother Pat was impregnated in high school and forced into a shotgun marriage with Michael's father, Dan Ross. Needless to say, they did not go on to lead a very happy marriage. Pat Ross was a very mentally unstable woman, who underwent two abortions and was institutionalized twice. She abandoned her children and family once to run off with another man, but she soon returned to a depressing and emotionally unhealthy life on the farm. Pat Ross seemed to resent Michael more than the other children. His sister claimed that Michael received the brunt of their mother's aggression. Michael Ross claimed that he didn't remember his dark childhood or his emotional abuse-ridden family; he only had fond memories of working on his father's farm. The joyous memories of working on the farm centered on his peculiar job; Michael's job was to ring the necks of sick and malnourished chickens.

He recalled that he began to experience sexual fantasies around this time, like most boys his age, but they weren't anything like the hellish compulsions he faced in his adulthood. He explained his boyish daydreams as non-violent, although they might've been considered peculiar by most. In an interview, Michael describes his early, innocent fantasies of women, "I would kidnap women and take them to my safe place, and then they would fall in love with me, and never want to leave." It has been said that Michael was molested as a child by his mentally ill uncle while babysitting. As an adult, Michael Ross claimed that he did not remember this incident or his uncle at all; Michael was only six years old when the suspected uncle committed suicide. Whether Michael was too young to recall the incident or if he merely repressed the memory, the irreparable damage that comes along with molestation could be a very influential part of Michael's slip into sexual sadism. Despite his strange desires, his dysfunctional family, and his history of abuse, Michael was considered to be a pretty average child. As a teenager, he excelled in school, graduating as number sixteen in his high school class, and he eventually moved to Cornell University to study Agriculture and Life Sciences.

College Years

He continued to excel academically throughout his years at university. He studied Economics, Agriculture, and Life Sciences, and excelled in all of his academic endeavors. He joined the FFA (Future Farmers of America) and the Alpha Zeta fraternity. Ross' sophomore year roommate and Alpha Zeta brother, described Ross in 1977, "He kind of followed his own drum and went his own way." Michael never made any real connections in his fraternity, nor did he really make connections to anyone besides the long string of girls that he dated. In his college year, Michael Ross was rarely without a girlfriend, and he was rarely thinking about anything but. "There was always a certain obsession on his part regarding women," said his Alpha Zeta roommate, "That seemed to be such a big issue, a constant topic—needing a woman, needing to have a girlfriend. He would be obsessed about the relationship."

Ross claims that he did not experience truly violent sexual fantasies until his years at Cornell University. He especially did not begin to fantasize about raping women until his sophomore year in college. Michael Ross said that somewhere in his undergraduate years, he began to embrace the desires that brewed within him. He started his downward spiral with a very small step. He began to stalk his fellow students on campus. He would follow close by, making it known that he was behind her. "I would get a thrill by them knowing that I was following them. That they would be scared and that gave me a thrill," Michael explained his early experimentation with his predatory nature. When simply stalking the women wasn't enough, Michael eventually turned to towards rape. He hid in the bushes of Beebe Lake and raped a visiting student. Later, he attempted to rape another girl outside of the school observatory but failed. These assaults were only stepping stones to the full-fledged horror that Michael Ross was destined to cause. During his senior year at Cornell University, Michael Ross met Dzung Ngoc Tu, a Vietnamese student, and his very first murder victim.

The case of Dzung Ngoc Tu perplexed officials everywhere. She was found on May 17, 1981, in the Fall Creek Gorge. She died from a skull fracture and her body laid there for five days until she was discovered. It appeared to be a suicide, as if she had jumped from the bridge overhead and hit her head upon the fall, but there was no suicide note left at the scene. Close friends and family of Dzung Ngoc Tu claimed that there absolutely no signs of suicidal tendencies when she was alive and investigators found absolutely no reason for killing herself. Her body showed no signs of sexual abuse, there were no suspects, and the police had no idea that the culprit was actually Michael Ross, a man who was only connected to her by their similar majors. The case went cold when the police couldn't find a suspect. It wasn't until Michael Ross was already in prison for the murders and rapes of four other women when he confessed to murdering and raping a Vietnamese girl that went to his school in New York.

The Attacks and Murders of The Roadside Strangler

Michael Ross chose his victims merely off of chance and circumstance. If he encountered a woman that was in a vulnerable position, he felt this undeniable compulsion to attack. "There's nothing they could've said or done. It was me, it wasn't them," Michael Ross admitted with a solemn tone of voice, years after his final attack, "They were dead as soon as I saw them, I think."

Michael claimed that he only attacked women to relieve pressure that built up from his personal relationships with the women in his life. When he was working in North Carolina, shortly after he graduated from college, Michael recalled that he had a very difficult visit from his fiancé, which caused him to attack a random woman shortly after he dropped his fiancé off at the airport. He noticed a woman walking on the sidewalk with a baby stroller, so Michael pulled the car over and attacked her, using her own child as a weapon. "I told her that if she didn't do what I wanted, I would smash the baby's head against the wall of the house," Michael described in an interview, he seemed as if he were on the verge of tears, "I've always said that I never understood why these women never really resisted me. I'm not a big, strong guy, but nobody ever seemed to fight. I've always just contributed it as I must say something like that, or similar to it, to the other victims." He raped and strangled the woman, then left her for dead in her driveway.

On June 15, 1982, a 23-year-old woman named Debra Smith Taylor was attacked by Michael Ross in a park. He pulled her over where no one could see them, raped her, and forced her to roll over on her stomach; he then strangled her from behind. The young girl's body was discovered much later in a dried up river bed, only a few miles away from the location of another of Ross' victims, Tammy L. Williams. "Each time I killed, I made myself believe that I wasn't going to kill again," Michael Ross explained in an interview. It wasn't very long before he killed again.

His next attack occurred on a cold Thanksgiving Day in 1983. Michael Ross encountered Robin Stavinsky outside of Norwich State Hospital. He saw the woman in a vulnerable position and he took advantage of the situation. He forced the 19-year-old girl into a wooded area and demanded her to remove her clothing. Ross forced himself on the young girl then told her to roll over on her stomach. He strangled her from behind until the innocent Robin Stavinksky died in his hands. "Serial killers like to strangle their victims and that is, I guess, the most common form of killing because there's more of a connection there. It's more real and it's not as quick," Michael Ross explained why he enjoyed strangling so much. After he was finished with her, he covered her body with leaves and left her for dead.

The Roadside Strangler struck again on Easter Sunday, 1984. April Brunias and Leslie Shelly were hitchhiking on the side of the road when Michael Ross happened to drive their way. He pulled over and offered the young girls a ride. The girls did not find Ross threatening so they got into his car and asked him to drop them off at the next gas station. When Michael passed the gas station, one of the girls drew a kitchen knife and threatened to stab him. In an interview Michael Ross explained what happened next, "I almost drove off of the road, I was so surprised. I don't know what I said, but I said something and she gave the knife to me. It obviously scared her." He parked the car at Beach Pond and used a cloth to bound both of the girls by their hands and feet. He put Leslie Shelly in the trunk of his car, then dragged the girl named April a few feet away from the car. He raped the young girl, flipped her over onto her stomach, and strangled her until she died. He then took Leslie out of the trunk and did the same thing to her. "The smallest one, Leslie Shelly, has always bothered me more than the others. I think it was because she was so small, I think it was because she was so cooperative, and I think it was because the way she was killed was so close to the fantasy. That was the one that was... it was like it was fantasy," Michael explained. The girls were only fourteen years old when they were murdered.

It was a summer afternoon, around three o'clock on June 13, 1984, when the Roadside Strangler committed the murder that would finally get him caught. He was driving home from work when he passed Wendy Baribeault, who was walking down the side of busy Route 12 in Libson, only a few miles away from his home. Michael Ross pulled the car over and began to speak to this 17-year-old girl; he repeatedly invited her to his company picnic. After a little bit of conversation, Michael forced the beautiful, young girl over a stone wall and into the woods. "When I attacked her, I don't believe that I was in control. I don't think I would've been able to stop," Michael Ross explained his mental state during this attack, "I didn't really feel anything. I knew what was going on and I saw what was going on, but it was more like watching an old film..." Michael then raped the innocent girl and strangled her, just like the others, then entombed her in the stone wall that lined the busy road. The road was so busy, in fact, that there were several eyewitnesses to the attack.

The Investigation of the Roadside Strangler

The police had absolutely no leads on the murderer (a.k.a. The Roadside Strangler) that had taken Connecticut by storm. That was until Wendy Baribeault's body was found. There were dozens of eye witnesses to her attack and composite drawings were created that matched the facial features of local Michael Bruce Ross. Witnesses also noted that the attacker was driving a blue Toyota. Michael Malchik, the investigator assigned to the case, compiled a list of several thousand blue Toyotas. This tiny bit of evidence eventually led investigators directly to Ross' house, which was only three miles away from the location of the crime scene. Michael allegedly dropped hints that he was the murderer upon speaking to the police. "It all had to end," Michael Ross explained. It wasn't long before Michael was called into an interview with police in 1984. After a few hours of grueling interrogation, Michael Bruce Ross confessed to all crimes that he'd committed in Connecticut, but left out the murders in New York. "It's a mystery to me to this day, but it's typical of him," stated Detective Malchik, "Here he is, confessing to six murders, and he thought enough ahead not to tell us about the New York ones. Looking back at it, it's obvious he was thinking of something. He was always thinking two steps ahead. He's got his own agenda, but I couldn't for the life of me tell you what it is."

When Michael confessed to the murders, he seemed very sorrowful and remorseful, but he claimed not to feel a blink of remorse, "I don't want to say that I don't have any remorse, it's just like they weren't real..." Michael explains his feelings towards hid victims in a later interview, "I can't see them as I was killing them, so when I say I don't have any remorse, that doesn't mean that I don't have any regrets, or wish that didn't happen, or there was something that I could do to bring them back or anything – I don't have any feelings towards them. I feel like I should be tormented by them - by what they look like when I was killing them – or tormented by what was happening immediately before I killed them – but none of that's there. None of that's there at all."

"The only time he said he was sorry, was that he was sorry for getting caught," Michael's arresting officer explained, "He (Michael Ross) told me matter-of-factly, he said, 'If you hadn't caught me, I would've just kept on killing, again.'" This eerie statement by itself was enough to put the Roadside Strangler to death immediately, but his strange nature kept investigators questioning his motives behind being so upfront and honest about his heinous crimes. Did he secretly want to get caught? Was this all part of some big plot to instill his insanity?

Anne Cournoyer, Michael's correction counselor, described his mannerisms as he spoke of the horrible crimes that he committed, "One minute he's very, you know, looks like he on the verge of crying, and the next minute he's sort of giggling nervously - or sadistically – you just really don't know. You think that maybe, it's out of nervousness, but he could be getting pleasure out of talking about it."

A full-scale investigation of Michael Bruce Ross' life led to the realization of his wavering mental stability. Michael Ross explained that he could never recall the faces of his victims, even directly after the murders, "You'd think that if you killed someone, you would have the face imprinted in your mind and that you wouldn't be able to get it out of your mind – I don't have that. I never had that," He explained, "The only faces I could see was what was in the newspapers a few days later when they were missing. You know, the high school pictures and 'anybody know where this girl is?' type of thing. When I think of them, that's the picture that I see. I don't see them as they were when I killed them. If you had stopped me right after and gave me a composite drawing of like twelve pictures - you know - some blondes, brunettes, whatever – I wouldn't have been able to pick them out. Even immediately after I killed them."

The names of all eight women were: Dzung Ngoc Tu (25), Paula Perrera (16), Tammy Williams (17), Debra Smith Taylor (23), Robin Stavinksy (19), April Brunias (14), Leslie Shelley (14), and Wendy Baribeault (17). He was only charged with the murders of the four Connecticut women because the murders of Dzung Ngoc Tu and Paula Perrera took place in New York. He was sentenced to death on July 6, 1987, but remained on death row for eighteen years after his sanity was called into question.

The Curious Case of Michael Bruce Ross

Michael spent the next eighteen years of his life caught in a battle of the Connecticut justice system. In court, a team of psychiatrists flocked to the defense of Mr. Michael Ross. After a parade of psychiatric evaluation, Michael was deemed mentally unwell, due to his dark childhood and his undeniable compulsions. Dr. Fred Berlin, the well-known co-founder of the Johns Hopkins Sexual Disorder Clinic, testified that Ross was struggling with a mental disorder called sexual sadism. Meaning that he gained sexual excitement from the pain and suffering of others. This discovery alone was not enough to save Ross' life, but Michael's claim to lose all self-control during the murders was enough to set back his execution date. Connecticut's state psychiatrist reluctantly agreed that Ross was not mentally capable enough to be responsible for his own actions, and therefore, it was not right to put him to death. Dr. Robert Miller wrote in a private letter, "I can't see how I could testify against psychopathology playing a sufficient role in defendant's behavior." Although this letter was never presented in court, Michael Ross' death sentence was overturned in 1994 and a new sentencing hearing was scheduled in 2000.

Michael Bruce Ross spent most of his time on death row writing about the mental disorder that took hold of his entire life. Michael claimed to have no control over his actions due to his compulsions. He described his sexual sadism as "a mental illness that drove me to rape and kill" and "made me physically unable to control my actions." During his time in prison, Michael still fell victim to his compulsions. It was impossible for him to control his sexual desires, so he spent the first few months of his incarceration reliving the murders. He claimed that he would fantasize these murders over and over again, hurting himself and causing sores from compulsive masturbation. It wasn't very long before he begged for some type of relief from his sexual desires, which came in the form of chemical castration. Ross was given medication that was designed to lower his testosterone levels and it finally relieved him from his sadistic compulsions. Thanks to this medication, Michael Bruce Ross was finally able to think clearly and he was able to see the true nature of his crimes.

The team of prosecutors naturally disagreed with the defense's attempts to lessen his blame. Prosecutors claimed that if he were unable to control his desires, he would've made less calculated attacks. It was reasonable to assume that Ross experienced these sexual desires constantly, which means that he probably experienced these feelings while in public places, or places where his actions could've been seen and reprimanded. Instead, Ross chose his victims very carefully, only acting when the girls were vulnerable and alone. Disproving the defenses' claims more so was the fact that Ross' hid their bodies after the attack, which further strengthened his blame and the case that he knew precisely what he was doing when he was doing it. "I'm not saying I wasn't there or it was multi-personality or any of that type of crap," Michael Ross later explained the strange fog he experienced while he murdered these innocent women, "I was there and I did it, but I wasn't one hundred percent there." To set light upon Mr. Michael Ross' guilt, Prosecutors relied on the "Policeman at the Elbow" test: would Ross have committed the crime even if a policeman had been standing next to him?

The defense team immediately disagreed with the statement that all of Ross' attacks were calculated and well thought out, considering the murder of Ms. Wendy B. who was murdered next to a busy road with several eyewitnesses, "When I attacked her, I don't believe I was in control. I don't think I could've stopped." Michael spoke about the murder that eventually resulted in his incarnation. "Could he control himself? Well, two juries rejected that," Detective Malchik recalls, "As the state's attorney said at the trial if Ross was so out of control, why didn't he just rape the girl in between the yellow lines of Route 12? He made it simple for the juries to understand."

John Blume, a professor at the Law school and co-founder of the Cornell Death Penalty Project, noted the how the jury in Ross' case did not take the opinions of the psychological experts seriously. "The thing that's disturbing," Professor Blume stated, "is that even when the experts all say your client is insane, juries will still reject it." Despite the team of psychologists on Ross' side, claiming that he was completely unable to stop himself from committing these monstrosities, the jury chose not to believe them.

Somewhere in the eighteen years of Michael Ross' incarceration, he decided that he did not deserve to live anymore. Shortly after Michael wrote a story called "It's Time for Me to Die", he reconnected with a woman named Kathy Jaeger, who served as his pastoral advocate that converted Ross to Catholicism. Ross wrote in a newsletter that Jaeger, "was able to breach my defenses and was able to touch my soul as no one else ever has." He later called Ms. Kathy Jaeger "the most important woman in my life" and claimed that "If I were a free man, I would ask her to marry me." Although Kathy rejects his claims to romance, she continued to support Michael Ross throughout his decisions.

After she entered Michael's life, there was a great shift in the nature of his case. Michael was done fighting for his life and the mental condition that wreaked havoc on his entire existence. After his original death sentence was overturned in 1994, the court ordered a new penalty hearing, but instead of going through the hearing with his public defenders, Ross acted as his own attorney. He worked with prosecutor C. Robert Satti to created what was deemed as "death pact" that allowed the imposition of the death penalty without a penalty hearing. "Please allow me to go into the courtroom . . . to accept the death penalty as punishment for my actions," Ross wrote in a letter to Satti. "I'm not asking you to do this for me, but for the families involved, who do not deserve to suffer further and who, in some small way, might gain a sense of peace of mind by these actions and my execution." The "death pact" was rejected by the judge as a "short cut" involving a human life, so Michael Ross flip-flopped back into his old ways. Ross returned to his defense team and reverted back into fighting for his life, claiming that his crimes were merely a product of his mental illness. He was resentenced to death soon after.

Jaeger said that Ross's sudden acceptance of death was a sincere attempt to provide closure for the families of his victims, "He told me, 'You know I don't want to do this. But I have to.' He just really felt anguish over what he had done. Really, really harsh anguish and self-loathing. Contrary to media reports, he doesn't want to die. He wishes that the justice system got it right years ago and gave him life sentences because he does have a mental illness. And the sad thing is, if they had done that, the families of his victims wouldn't have been re-victimized [by the ongoing appeals]. Michael is trying, in essence, to save them from any more of that."

Whether his acceptance of the death sentence was sincere, or not, Michael Bruce Ross was sentenced to death by lethal injection on May 13, 2005. He chose not to speak any last words before his death and died peacefully in the execution chair. Some family members believed that his death was too peaceful. Debbie Dupuis, Robin Stavinsky's sister, stated that she thought she would "feel closure" but instead just "felt anger" as she watched Ross simply lay there, go to sleep and die.

The state of Connecticut finally decided to end the life of the Roadside Strangler and put an end to the anguish that the families had to endure. After a very tragic and dark lifetime, Michael Bruce Ross and his sadistic compulsions were finally laid to rest.

Conclusion

Michael Bruce Ross is the type of cold, calculating, manipulative killer that we only read about in horror novels. His crimes almost seem too heartless and brutal to be true, but the victims of the Roadside Strangler would tell you that he is nothing but a cruel reality. In only a few years, Michael assaulted a countless number of women and murdered eight. Although he was only charged with four murders, Ross was forced to withstand eighteen long years of debate over his life sentence. In prison, he transitioned from a vicious killer who was truly non-remorseful for his brutal crimes to a man who seemed to genuinely regret his life choices and the pain that he subjected. Towards the end of his life, Ross begged for removal from his troubled existence, not only for himself but to end the long and grueling process of the legal system. Despite his transition into humanity, Michael Bruce Ross never took full blame for his actions. He flip-flopped between blaming his childhood, his compulsions, and his interpersonal relationships for these terrible crimes. He claimed to never feel any guilt or remorse for his actions, simply because he wasn't completely there while they were taking place. During these attacks, Michael claims that he was under some type of spell, some type of fog that completely disconnected him from his actions. He was completely able to murder and rape these innocent women without feeling guilt or remorse, or even being able to recall the very faces of his victims', only moments after their attack. Michael Ross was an extremely troubled man who suffered from a very extreme case of sexual sadism. Michael explained his cruel, heartless, attacks with vivid details and an undetached tone of voice. The scariest part about his calm demeanor is the monotone way that he described the way he stole the lives of these young, innocent women. He speaks as if he were not responsible for killing these beautiful and young women, although he willingly confesses to the murders. He claimed that he was merely a victim of his sexual compulsions since his college years and the women he attacked were merely in the wrong place at the wrong time. Whether his desires were really uncontrollable or if it was merely an excuse, Michael Bruce Ross' case remains to be one of the most perplexing cases in American history. His mere mental condition was enough to perplex the entire state of Connecticut – how could this well-spoken, articulate man with such a great personality, commit these terrible crimes? Why didn't anyone notice his decline and stop it? What was it that made this seemingly normal man snap into the Roadside Strangler? Although the answers to these questions are uncertain, they definitely are unnerving. Michael Ross was created by circumstances, by his dark upbringing, and a lifetime of people letting him slip through the cracks. Everyone saw him as an average, everyday college student, so no one thought to ask. The woman that he murdered were sadly only stepping stones into the downward spiral into his sickness and they were eventually caused the end of his vicious, murderous cycle.

STOCKWELL STRANGLER : The True Story of Kenneth Erskine

NATALIE MARSHALL

Kenneth Erskine, known as "The Stockwell Strangler" due to the geographic proximities of his murders, was a deeply troubled young man who had demonstrated worrisome signs of violence and schizophrenia from a young age. He was a gerontophile in that he had an unnatural sexual attraction to the elderly. Gerontophilia, essentially, is the opposite of pedophilia. Erskine would break into elderly men's and women's London flats and strangle them while they were in bed; after which he would rape and/or sodomize most of them. To demonstrate his own warped sense of love for his victims he would cross their arms across their chest, close their eyes, and tuck them into bed. Also, perhaps to hide his shame, he would turn his victims' family photographs face down. There was much speculation among mental health professionals that Erskine also suffered from schizophrenia from a very young age.

He was eventually convicted of seven murders and one attempted murder and sentenced to life in prison in 1988 at the age of 25. However, in July 2009, following an appeal his murder convictions were reduced to manslaughter on the grounds of diminished capacity and he received a hospital order to serve his life sentences at Broadmoor Hospital. While he has the potential to be granted parole in 2028, the trial judge's original order was that Erskine should spend at least 40 years behind bars, thus making him at least 65 years of age before potential eligibility for release.

Early Life

Kenneth Erskine was born in Hammersmith, London in July 1963. His mother Margaret was British and his father Charles was from Antigua. He was one of four boys, had an average IQ when tested at eight years old, and was remembered by neighbors to be a "chubby, Bible reading soul"; however, he became increasingly violent and difficult to control. For example, as a child, Erskine had tried to hang his younger brother, John, twice.

Erskine was then sent to a series of schools for maladjusted and troubled children where he received his formal education. He frequently and violently attacked his teachers and classmates and was identified as inhabiting a fantasy world with murderous impulses. In his own private fantasy world he would take on the role of Lawrence of Arabia, attacking and tying up smaller and weaker children—a theme that would resurface when he targeted the weaker elderly during his murder spree. During a school-sponsored swimming outing he had attempted to drown several classmates by holding their heads under the water until teachers were forced to intervene. He set fires at school and once pushed a classmate off of a moving bus. On another occasion he stabbed a teacher in the hand with a pair of scissors. In another event, a psychiatric nurse who tried to examine Erskine was taken hostage by him as he held a pair of scissors to her throat. He strangled the classroom guinea pig. Whenever any female staff tried to be empathetic and show him any type of affection he would expose his genitals or rub up against them.

There was frequent talk that Erskine demonstrated clear signs and symptoms of schizophrenia as a teenager but nothing ever came out of it. He never had therapy or medication or any real psychiatric evaluation.

By the time Erskine was 16 years of age he had turned to drugs and particularly enjoyed inhalants. This latest display of misbehavior was too much for his mother who eventually kicked him out of the house, forcing him to survive on his own. When Erskine tried to give his younger brother marijuana she finally disowned him. He never saw any of his family members ever again and was forced to spend the next seven years of his life "drifting through the twilight world of London's homeless and rootless" living in squats and hostels in Brixton and Stockwell and getting involved with petty crime which primarily took the shape of failed burglaries on primarily the elderly.

Erskine's violent tendencies continued to worsen.

When he was 18 he stabbed a young male with whom he was having a homosexual relationship at the time. Erskine had burst into his boyfriend's bedroom and stabbed and slashed at his body while he lay in bed. Whereas this may have been the first attack of someone in bed it was a glaring omen of the terror he would wreak in six years.

Erskine was described my many who knew him as a persistent loner who drifted through life and due to no direction of any type of social support system started a life of crime. Erskine was also a Rastafarian due to his Caribbean heritage but was shunned by fellow Rastafarians due to his habit of theft.

An unsuccessful burglar, he was jailed on many occasions.

Among Erskine's favorite "drugs" were solvents—such as glue—which he would inhale. Among the most oft-cited short term effects of huffing glue are hallucinations, delusions, and hostility. Long-term effects include depression, irritability, memory impairment, diminished intelligence, and serious and sometimes irreversible brain damage. There continues to be speculation as to whether Erskine was born with his psychopathic tendencies (nature) or whether his upbringing and environmental stimuli were to blame for his problems (nurture). The consensus is that a combination of factors worked together to create Erskine's sick and murderous persona.

Erskine subsequently spent considerable time in Borstals—youth detention centers—due to being apprehended following his many failed burglaries. While in one for burglary in 1982 Erskine would paint and draw pictures of elderly people in bed with gags in their mouths, with daggers in them, or burned to death. Additional pieces of "artwork" included headless figures with blood spurting out from their necks, people holding human hearts in their hands, disemboweled people, screaming faces, and copious pools of blood. Again, this was a chilling omen of what was to come. In one documentary about Kenneth Erskine and his crimes, one of his cellmates at Borstal, named James, described how horrific Erskine's paintings were and how he would frequently smile and laugh while painting them. As Erskine's only "friend" James became his confidant as well. The two would play chess to pass the time and then there were Erskine's disturbing paintings. James stated in an interview that Erskine always spoke very quietly—rarely above a whisper—and was very weird.

Borstal doctors were concerned enough to the point of asking the authorities not to ever free Erskine because they were seriously worried that he might try to replicate his paintings; however, he was, in fact, released and four years later he would begin his killing spree.

The Crimes

At some point Erskine decided to act out his fantasies and began to murder. He is classified as a geographically-stable serial killer who confined his murders to a specific area. As Erskine had no vehicle and roamed around the Stockwell area frequently confining his murders to this area was likely due to simple necessity.

The Stockwell section of South London is a favored place for the elderly to retire. In the summer of 1986, however, a serial killer conducted a reign of terror throughout the community that resulted in seven known deaths—and possibly another four—attributable to The Stockwell Strangler.

Eileen Nancy Emms, 78

Emms was a 78-year-old retired schoolteacher who lived in an "unkempt basement flat" on West Hill Road in Wandsworth. She was sexually assaulted and strangled by Erskine on 6 April 1986.

Emms' body was found on 9 April 1987 by her home help who, upon knocking on her bedroom door and receiving no response one morning, let herself in to find Emms in bed with the covers pulled up to her chin, seemingly asleep. There were no obvious marks upon her body. Initially, the cause of death was attributed to natural causes. The doctor called to the scene estimated that she died approximately three days earlier and signed a death certificate that stated natural causes.

Once the victim's home help noticed that her small portable television was missing, the police were called.

During her autopsy, the medical examiner revealed that Emms had been strangled by bare hands. There was heavy bruising to her chest which strongly suggested that her assailant had kneeled atop her while strangling her. Further examination revealed that she had been sodomized as the assailant had left semen around her anus.

A short Afro-Caribbean head hair was found on her sheet.

Janet Crockett, 67

Janet Crockett was Erskine's first July 1987 victim. She was chairwoman of her local tenant's association. Her body was found on 9 June in her flat in the Overton Estate in Stockwell. She had been strangled but, unlike Erskine's first victim—and subsequent ones—she was not sexually assaulted.

Police were able to immediately conclude that she had been murdered as she had considerable bruising on her chest due to sustaining two broken ribs as a result of someone kneeling on her while she was strangled to death. Additionally, her nightgown had been ripped from her body and folded neatly and placed upon a bedside chair.

Police also noticed that framed family photographs on the bedroom mantel had been placed face down or turned around. This action would be repeated at several of his crime scenes and speculation abounds as to what Erskine's underlying motive for doing this was. Some psychological experts have surmised that his anger at his own parents' rejection without a healthy outlet for his emotions led to an insane jealousy of normal family ties. Another hypothesis was that he felt ashamed at his actions and didn't want any "witnesses."

Police were able to find a smudged thumbprint on a displaced planter and a palm print on the bathroom window.

Pathologist Dr. Iain West conducted Crockett's autopsy and compared it to Emms. He concluded that their methods of strangulation were similar. He stated that with weaker elderly victims unconsciousness would occur within 30 second and death after approximately three minutes. While Crockett's and Emms' murders were similar—and that they were both elderly—police had nothing else to link the two victims.

Frederick Prentice, 73

In the early hours of 27 June, 73-year-old retired engineer Frederick Prentice was asleep in his council-run elderly people's home on Cedars Road in Clapham when he was awakened by the sounds of someone entering his bedroom. He saw a young man enter and Prentice turned on his bedside lamp and ordered the intruder to leave. Erskine then pounced atop the old man, placed his index finger to his own mouth as a threat for Prentice to be quiet, and then sat upon his chest where he alternated squeezing his windpipe powerfully, then relaxing his grip, and repeated this multiple times. Prentice told police that his assailant had whispered only one word over and over: "Kill." Prentice was able to push the alarm button near his bed which caused his assailant to leave.

After talking to Prentice the police were fairly confident that all of the victims thus far were, in fact, linked. A shoeprint found at the scene would also serve to connect this attack with some of the other murders.

Prentice would later identify Erskine in a lineup.

Valentine Gleim, 84, and Zbigniew Stabrawa, 94

The next day Erskine murdered 84-year-old World War II veteran Valentine Gleim and 94-year-old Polish immigrant Zbigniew Stabrawa in their adjoining rooms at Somerville Hastings House, an old folks' home on Stockwell Park Crescent. Both men had been manually strangled and sodomized.

The intruder had been seen by alert night duty staff but had vanished before the police arrived. Point of entry was, again, determined to be an open window. Staff were also able to see Erskine fleeing the scene and estimated his height at approximately five-feet-eight-inches with a slim frame so at least now investigators had a clue about their suspect.

Of particular concern in these two cases was the discovery of a used flannel towel and electric shaver which suggested that the murderer had calmly washed up and shaved after killing two people.

Approximately one hour prior to the double homicide an elderly woman in a Stockwell old folks' home was attacked while she was in bed by a man grabbing her arm. She fought off her assailant so vehemently that he had to run off. Her description of Erskine matched Prentice's.

William Carmen, 82

Two weeks after his previous double homicide, Erskine struck again by strangling and sexually assaulting 82-year-old widower William Carmen on 8 July. This time he threw a monkey wrench at detectives by murdering on the other side of the Thames river, in Islington, North London. Carmen was discovered dead in his bed in his flat on the Marques Estate by his daughter. As was the case with Erskine's other victims, Carmen was in bed with the covers pulled up neatly to his chin and had been sodomized.

This time there was clear evidence of ransacking and theft as approximately £400 of Carmen's savings was missing. Family photos were also placed face down or turned around.

William Downes, 74

On 20 July the body of 74-year-old William Downes was found by his son in his Holles House on Overton Road flat in Brixton; the same location where Erskine's second victim, Crockett, lived. He was naked and in bed with the covers pulled up to his chin, his eyes closed, and his arms folded across his chest—classic Erskine signature. Downes' son had reminded him to keep his windows locked firmly at night a few days ago so as not to fall victim to the Strangler but he failed to heed these instructions and point of entry was, again, determined to be through an unlocked window.

Downes had been strangled and sexually assaulted like the majority of Erskine's other victims. There were semen stains on the sheets.

Investigators lifted a palm print from the kitchen wall and another from the garden gate which were eventually matched to the prints found at Crockett's home. Finding the owner of these prints, however, was not as easy as the process is today. In 1986, while fingerprints were on file on computer discs at

Scotland Yard, palm prints were not. Investigators had a stack of four million files; however, by concentrating on London-based burglars and petty thieves, they were able to compile a more workable load. They were subsequently able to match the prints to those Erskine, a small-time crook with an extensive rap sheet for burglary.

Unfortunately, the police did not know where to find Erskine and while they were looking he struck again, killing his final victim.

Florence Tisdall, 80

80-year-old partially blind and deaf Florence Tisdall was found in her apartment at Ranelagh Gardens near Putney Bridge on 24 July. The caretaker of the apartments noticed her walker in the communal corridor and knew something was wrong as Tisdall was unable to get around without it. He found her strangled, sexually assaulted, and with broken ribs as a result of her killer sitting atop her chest. She had spent the previous day watching the televised wedding of the Duke and Duchess of York—Prince Andrew and Sarah Ferguson—even having her own hair done especially for the big event. Tisdall had lived in an almost empty block of flats where she had resided for the past 60 years. A cat lady, she had left her windows open so the cats could come and go as they pleased and this is how Erskine got into her flat.

It was at this scene where Erskine made, perhaps, his biggest mistake. Detectives knew immediately that Tisdall had been murdered because she was found in her nightgown, tucked into bed with the covers up by her chin. In reality, however, Tisdall's neighbors who frequently checked on her because of her disabilities stated that she always slept atop the covers in the clothing she had been wearing that day. When Erskine undressed Tisdall to rape her, he attempted to cover up his misdeeds by making it look as though she went to bed as usual and died of natural causes. Family photos were also placed face down or turned around as was the case at the Crockett crime scene.

One of Tisdall's neighbors stated that she saw Erskine near the victim's flat shortly after the murder had occurred "looking disgusted with himself." Thinking this to be odd she promptly notified the police.

All of Erskine's victims were pensioners and in all but one case there was evidence of sexual assault that took the form of sodomy; however, investigators and forensic specialists cannot say whether it occurred before or after the victims' death.

Investigation and Arrest

After the Crockett murder, Scotland Yard's Serious Crimes Squad Detective Chief Superintendent Ken Thompson—a Scotsman with 26 years' experience—was put in charge of the case and given over 200 detectives to devote to the search for The Stockwell Strangler. Interestingly, Erskine was originally nicknamed "The Heatwave Killer" because the murders occurred during the summer; however, when the majority of his murders occurred in and around Stockwell this nickname was changed. Further, plainclothes officers would stand guard throughout the night wherever the elderly lived.

At the height of the investigation, as many as 350 law enforcement officers were on the Strangler case which included 150 detectives and senior officers from the C1 Murder Squad who worked out of five separate incident rooms throughout London which were linked to a special Home Office computer. This network was called HOLMUS and was used to prevent wasting time by cross checking paperwork which proved to be detrimental to the investigation for Peter Sutcliff, The Yorkshire Ripper. Other police officers set up fixed observation points in neighborhoods with a high population of elderly residents and instituted extra patrols.

A psychologist was enlisted to create a profile of the Strangler and to provide potential insight into his signature to determine whether he was attempting to cover his tracks or was fulfilling some bizarre fantasy. The suspect was determined to be suffering from gerontophilia; or a sexual attraction to the elderly and the complete opposite of its better known opposite, pedophilia. Speculation abounded as to whether the killer's sexual paraphilia was a result of some relationship problems with his grandparents. Additionally, as his victims were all selected at random, authorities could not link the victims together with the hopes of finding some commonality between them that would enable them to identify and apprehend the man responsible.

The suspect was classified as a process-focused serial killer. The majority of serial killers are of this type; the other being act-focused wherein their own psychological gratification from the kill itself is the underlying cause. Instead, process-focused killers achieve a hedonistic psychological "reward." These types frequently "get off" on the method of their kill and they enjoy the perverse sexual thrill that accompanies the act of killing. The literature identifies four types of process-focused serial killers: gain in which the killer kills for profit or personal gain; thrill in which the act of killing gives the killer a rush or a high; power in which the killer enjoys dominating and manipulating victims and while sex is usually involved it is primarily tertiary to the kill itself; and lust wherein murder is associated with sexual pleasure and this type of killer will commonly have sex while in the process or killing or may engage in necrophilia after death. As far as Erskine is concerned, he can be classified in multiple subtypes. First, since he did rob his victims and steal money he demonstrates some elements of the gain process-focused serial killer. Secondly, he did obtain a rush or high from killing his victims and, therefore, does demonstrate some elements of a thrill killer. This element is particularly salient when he was seen by a witness—who would later testify against him—getting sick on the sidewalk after his final kill near where his last victim was found. The act of his getting sick appears to be directly attributed to the thrill her received from killing and having sex with his victim. Finally, since Erskine likely sodomized his victims after he killed them his sexual fantasies were of a higher priority than is typically the case for power killers. Thus, he demonstrates elements more aligned with a lust killer.

Coupled with the fact that Erskine targeted the same type of people and that he engaged in specific rituals which were part of his signature makes Erskine a classic serial killer. His smaller size likely contributed to his choice of the elderly as his victims because in their weakened conditions he wouldn't have much trouble overpowering them.

The palm prints were the most damning evidence investigators had at that point; however, they only placed Erskine at two of the murder scenes. Despite similarities among all of the victims' crime scenes, the fact that Erskine wasn't cooperating with police required detectives to find other evidence. Investigators from Scotland Yard took the unusual step of distributing his Erskine's picture to the media to try to find more witnesses and potential leads by hopefully jog people's memories as to whether anyone may remember seeing him. Thompson also did something very uncommon; he appeared on television, appealing to Erskine to turn himself in.

After Tisdall's death the search for Erskine intensified even more than was already the case; however, being that he was a drifter with no permanent address or any real belongings to speak of they had to search through the hundreds of hostels and squats in South London. His life was so devoid of meaning and friends to help detectives find him.

Investigators got their big break when they realized that since the suspect was likely unemployed that he would be receiving social security and unemployment benefits. Upon further investigation they discovered that Erskine picked up his benefits on alternating Mondays from a Department of Health and Social Security office in Southwark, South London, and that he was due to collect his next check on 28 July. The building was placed under surveillance and when Erskine turned up, right on time, he was arrested and handcuffed without any struggle.

Whereas items and cash from the victims' homes were, in fact, missing, police did not believe that robbery was the driving motive in the homicides. There were neither signs of struggle nor any signs of forced entry. Police surmised that Erskine entered the flats through unsecured windows.

Forensic evidence linking the cases relied upon the fact that the victims were all murdered in similar ways: by the assailant kneeling on the victims' chests and then placing his left hand over their mouths and strangling them with his right hand. The semen collected at nearly all crime scenes suggested the same genetic fingerprint in that the same suspect was responsible for all of the sexual assaults. Additionally, there was a single hair found in Emms' flat, as well as matching shoeprints from three of the scenes.

A hairdresser informed investigators that Erskine had approached her wanting his head and pubic hair bleached. While she agreed to the former she refused the latter. Apparently, while he was sitting in the shop waiting for the bleach to take effect he self-applied the bleach to his pubic region and eyebrows, the latter resulting in his getting chemicals in his eyes and requiring assistance in washing it out.

When questioned by Detective Inspector Brian Jackson and other detectives, Erskine's responses indicated that the detectives' jobs were to be much more difficult than they thought. Erskine spent the majority of the interrogation giggling, staring out of the window or into the sky, or masturbating. After he was arrested, psychologists placed Erskine's mental age at 11 even though he was 24 at the time. He had first denied that he was, indeed, The Stockwell Strangler claiming instead to be a petty burglar who had no motive to kill anyone. After vehemently denying his culpability and blameworthiness in the string of murders and seeing that he wasn't getting anywhere, Erskine then changed his tune and said, "I don't remember killing anyone. I could have done it without knowing it. I am not sure if I did it." He also tried to blame the murders on a whispering female voice in his head. He once stated, "It tries to think for me. It says it will kill me if it gets me," and, "It blanks things from my mind."

He was clearly disturbed but not a fool in any sense. In fact, when searched, detectives found ten bank and building society accounts that Erskine had opened to hide the proceeds of his crimes. During the three-month span of murders, he had deposited over £3,000; quite a large sum of money for someone who was unemployed. This included a £350 deposit into one of his accounts on the morning after the Carmen murder. It was evident at this point that Erskine was amassing profits from his burglaries while simultaneously collecting unemployment benefits. This demonstrated that whereas Erskine did suffer from some degree of mental retardation and likely some psychosexual paraphilia he was not stupid by any means. In fact, he told detectives that his motive was to achieve notoriety. He said, "I wanted to be famous ... I thought I would never get caught."

During a lineup—or identity parade as it is called in England—surviving victim Frederick Prentice was able to definitively identify Erskine. Another woman who had witnessed Erskine vomiting on the sidewalk near Putney Bridge a mere 200 yards from the scene of the final murder on the night in question also picked Erskine out of a lineup.

Trial and Conviction

Erskine's trial commenced at the Old Bailey on 12 January 1988. He pled not guilty to the charges of seven murders and the attempted murder of Prentice. During his trial he would stare out the window or down at his feet as was the case when he was interrogated. When details of the murders were brought up, Erskine would masturbate.

The jury heard him confess to the burglaries of the deceased victims; however, he claimed that someone else must have followed him and killed the individuals after he had left. Nobody was buying this story.

After an 18-day trial, the jury unanimously found him guilty on all eight counts and he was sentenced to seven life terms plus 12 years for attempted murder with a recommended minimum of 40 years; one of the heaviest penalties ever handed out in British legal history. However, diagnosis of schizophrenia and other mental illnesses pursuant to the Mental Health Act of 1983 led to a successful appeal of Erskine's murder charges which were eventually reduced to manslaughter. He is currently serving his time at the Broadmoor Hospital.

In addition to his seven known victims, the police suspected Erskine of four other murders for which he has never been charged due to insufficient evidence to prove that he was, in fact, the murderer.

John Jordan, 57

On 4 February 1986, 57-year-old John Jordan was found in his Josephine Avenue flat in Brixton strangled beside his bed.

Charles Quarrell, 73

73-year-old Charles Quarrell was found suffocated in his bed on King James Street in Suffolk on 6 May. He had two handkerchiefs stuffed into the back of his throat, effectively blocking his windpipe.

Wilfred Parkes, 70

70-year-old Wilfred Parkes was found on 28 May in his Stockwell flat, suffocated and in bed. A nearby pillow was presumed to have been the murder weapon.

Trevor Thomas, 75

On 12 July 75-year-old Trevor Thomas was found dead in the bath at his home on Barton Court, Clapham. As Thomas had been dead for quite a while there was inadequate forensic evidence for investigators to link his murder to the others; thus resulting in Erskine not being charged with his death even though Thomas was almost certainly one of his victims.

As mentioned, Erskine has never been charged with these additional deaths; however, police were so confident that Erskine murdered them that they effectively closed the book on all of these cases. There is also much speculation that he likely killed prior to his first known victim—such as was the case with Mr. Jordan—and that because of his choice of victims their deaths may have simply been attributed to natural causes.

Aftermath

There is not much more information on Erskine due to a lack of any detailed studies of him as is commonly the case with other serial killers where the literature is rife with speculation as to what influences led to the individual turning to serial murder. His only possessions were meager clothes and some books from the building society. Other than a post-arrest diagnosis of schizophrenia, the mind of Kenneth Erskine remains mostly shrouded in mystery. In fact, his mentally-disturbed state has worsened to the point where he has been told that he will never be released from Broadmoor Hospital.

Psychiatrists have never been able to fully penetrate his mind and discover what makes him tick. He clearly has a problem differentiating fantasy from reality and appears to be locked in his own childlike world. However, there is one incident that clearly demonstrates his understanding between right and wrong. On 23 February 1996, Erskine prevented the possible murder of Peter Sutcliffe, known as the "Yorkshire Ripper" by alerting guards while another inmate, Paul Wilson, attempted to strangle Sutcliffe with the flexible cord from a pair of stereo headphones. Erskine was able to restrain Wilson from inflicting further injury upon Sutcliffe until guards arrived.

Erskine found himself on the receiving end of an assault. On Christmas Eve in 1997 he was attacked by fellow inmate, 34-year-old Keith Hanger. Hanger was serving time for the 1992 shooting of his friend after having escaped from prison. He walked up to Erskine and squirted liquid from an aerosol can into his face before lighting it with a lighter. Erskine was taken to Frimley Park Hospital in Surrey, in agonizing pain and worried that he would lose his eyesight; however, his temporary blindness was just that—temporary.

Psychiatrists continue to attempt to probe Erskine's mind trying to uncover more and more of his psyche toward, perhaps, finding what makes him tick. Currently, he is unable to answer for his crimes, as demonstrated by the reduced sentence due to diminished capacity.titutes during the interrogation, which would explain why his DNA was found on three of the young girls' bodies. He focused on Tania Nichols, telling a story about how he picked her up with the intention to have sexual relations, but changed his mind and returned her back to the red light district. Again, this account differed from the one that he originally gave to investigators. On February 21, 2008, Steve Wright was charged as guilty on all five counts of murder after eight hours of deliberation. He received a life sentence without any chance of parole. On February 22, 2008, Wright was taken to prison, where he'll be forced to live out the rest of his years behind bars.

Wright is still alive to this day and he is having a terrible time in prison. His twisted state of mind after imprisonment is outlined in his letter to his father: "...I just wish everyone would get along and work towards a family unit because all the bickering and point scoring against each other is really getting me down it seems you are pulling me one way and pam is pulling me the other and in the end, something will give and it just seems to me that person will be me and that is the last thing that I want at the moment has I am sure you do as well because if I start to fall apart at the seams I don't think I could cope in here I need to be strong to cope with this nightmare like that but you said in the paper that when you looked [in] my eyes you would know whether I was guilty or not that really hurt me it was like a knife in the heart for you to even contemplate that I could even be capable of such a terrible crime. You say you want to help me the only way that will happen is if you make the effort to work together because all this he said she said you must understand is not doing my frame of mind any good I just want it to stop I do love you dad..."